JAZ

I AM HUMAN
Pain & Pleasure

Martin Johnson

THINK YOU WILL LOVE
THIS ONE,
LOTS OF LOVE
MARTIN
xxx

big
ideas
library®

Published by Big Ideas Library 2024
Copyright © Martin Johnson, 2024
Martin Johnson has asserted his right to be identified as the
author of this work.

First published in the United Kingdom in 2024
by Big Ideas Library.

Big Ideas Library
20 Fountayne Street, York YO31 8HL
A CIP catalogue record for this book is available from the
British Library.
ISBN 978-1-7384604-2-7

Edited by Jacky Fitt
Design and illustrations by Ned Hoste
Printed by CPI Group (UK)

Big Ideas Library is the publishing division of
The Big Ideas Collective Ltd.

For Lucy

You continue to be the engine behind my driving force. I love you and thank you for your unwavering belief and support. xx

For Isabel, Nyla and Zander

When life seems difficult or out of balance, read this book and I will be with you. Dad xx

Foreword

In an era where technology increasingly intermediates our interactions with the world and each other, the release of this book couldn't be timelier. As we navigate through the accelerating pace of change and the complex tapestry of modern life, the question of what it means to be fundamentally human becomes more pertinent. This work is not just a book; it's a journey – an exploration into the depths of human nature, our behaviours, and the intrinsic needs that define our very existence.

From the moment that I first met him, Martin Johnson impressed me. He is a unique breed of person – one that marries lived experience with deep intelligence but in a way that relates, not pontificates. Martin's rich background spanning military service, business and leadership consultancy, brings a unique perspective. His transition from observing human behaviour in high-stakes environments to a broader contemplation on our collective psychological well-being reflects a concern for the state of humanity. At the heart of this concern lies a paradox: as our world grows more connected and affluent, why does our mental health seem to be in decline? This book dares to delve into these complexities, armed with insights gleaned from extensive experience and research.

Through a multidisciplinary lens that includes insights from evolutionary biology, psychology, and sociology, *I Am Human: Pain & Pleasure* embarks on a quest to uncover what lies beneath the surface of our actions and decisions. This exploration is anchored in the works of historical and contemporary thinkers, from Darwin to Freud, Jung, and beyond, weaving a narrative that is both enlightening and deeply human.

What sets this work apart is not just its ambitious scope but its accessibility. Martin's ability to distil complex concepts into relatable insights ensures that this book resonates with a broad audience. From leaders and professionals to anyone seeking to understand the intricacies of human behaviour, this book offers valuable perspectives.

As we stand on the brink of new technological frontiers, the message of this book is clear: to navigate the future successfully, we must look inward. We must understand the fundamental aspects of our nature and how they interact with the world we've built around us. This is not just a book about human behaviour; it's a guide to living a more conscious, connected, and human life in an increasingly digitised world.

At its core, it's a call to action. A reminder that, despite our advancements, we remain unquestionably human. It encourages us to reassess our relationship with technology, our environment and each other, to live lives that are not just successful in the conventional sense but are also fulfilling and meaningful.

Martin's work is exceptional. Not only is he a brilliant thinker and businessman, but most importantly he is a phenomenal human being, whether as a co-worker, a business partner, a family man or friend.

When Martin speaks or writes, I pay attention and so should everyone else.

Rich Diviney
Retired Navy SEAL and bestselling Author of *The Attributes*.
Owner and Founder of The Attributes Inc.

Why this book? Why now?

After spending my early years in the military, followed by 14 years in the world of business and management consultancy, in 2015 I founded my own learning and development consultancy, Trans2 Performance, known today as T2. In 2018 I wrote my first book *I Am Human: 30 Mistakes to Success* looking at the detail and impact of human behaviour. Throughout this time I have spent thousands of hours working with people and teams from all walks of life studying their behaviour and performance. The data I have collected and assessed through research, psychometric testing, observation and conversation has provided a fascinating insight into human behaviour, particularly against a background of a fast-emerging mental health crisis in rising- and high-income countries around the world.

At T2 we support organisations with culture, leadership development and performance psychology; primarily developing leaders to be more self-aware, to mobilise and motivate teams and create more engaging workplaces. We underpin everything we do with psychology. Our online platform has over 9000 users and rising, but most importantly, I have spent tens of thousands of hours being exposed to every single high-performance environment you can imagine. I've coached leaders of large global organisations, I've been at the forefront of elite sports in cycling, football and rugby, and experienced these unique high-performance, high-pressure environments. I've worked with emergency services personnel, such as Fire and Rescue, Police and the NHS, and have witnessed first-hand the pressure they are under on the front line, how their brains perform under that pressure, and ultimately the impact it has on their behaviours and mindset.

The T2 team and I have also conducted tens of thousands of team development and executive coaching sessions in all sorts of personal and professional situations. Capturing thousands of data points from surveys and assessments in leadership 360s and interviews, to date we've collected over 30,000 data points on our database. Through this, overseen by an occupational psychologist, we have developed a highly compelling picture of how humans and teams operate in modern-day society. All the theoretical modelling in the world is no substitute for getting out there and observing, understanding and capturing the realities of pressure, performance and how people function. What I look for is scientific, observable evidence gathered in real time, cross-referenced with the leading research and data from the worlds of neuroscience and psychology and, guess what? We're still learning.

Drawing from and building on the work of Charles Darwin, Sigmund Freud and Carl Jung, Yuval Noah Harari's *Sapiens*, Steve Peters' *The Chimp Paradox* and Maslow's Hierarchy of Needs, we continue to build an evolving picture of human behaviour, supercharged by recent leaps in our technological capability and societal and environmental shift. Each generation is faced with their own unique challenges but share the same biological and evolutionary footprint, and this is what fascinates me the most.

Through my observations, the overarching questions for me are:

"What does a happy and fulfilled human existence look and feel like and why do so many, who appear to have so much, exhibit greater rates of anxiety and depression than ever before?

"What's going on and, most importantly, is there an opportunity to get back to being human?"

In this book I'm going to explore some of our most basic human instincts and how these play out in our modern-day world. Could our greatest evolutionary asset now be our biggest challenge? And now, more than ever, can we reset our relationship with our ourselves, our environment and each other to live more fulfilled and purposeful lives?

Buckle up, were going in...

Introduction: Are You Sitting Comfortably? 11

Chapter 1. Unquestionably Human 13

Chapter 2. Pain and Pleasure 27

Chapter 3. Nature and Nurture 44

Chapter 4. Your World View 61

Chapter 5. Enduring Pain 70

Chapter 6. Seeking Pleasure 84

Chapter 7. Generational Shift 101

Chapter 8. Your World View Revisited 121

Chapter 9. Balancing the Scales 139

Chapter 10. The Future 174

Acknowledgements 185

About the Author 186

If you have enjoyed this book 187

Endnotes 188

Further Reading 195

Are You Sitting Comfortably? Most of us are not.

Good mental health is under siege and the taking of anti-anxiety medication is on the rise across the world, predominantly in countries with high and rising income levels. Given this increasing wealth and comfort, why are so many of us in so much pain?

In this book I'm going to explore the psychology of pain and pleasure and explain how it governs everything we do. For thousands of years we have survived and evolved through our ability to endure pain and suffering and adapt accordingly. This ability, combined with purpose, fulfilment and pleasure, has been the key to our species' dominance and success. Yet today we find ourselves in murky waters. The scales have tipped, and the psychological balance is out of kilter.

I'll explore the biological and evolutionary reasons behind pain and pleasure, and how these manifest as need, desire, anxiety and stress, remembering that some pain isn't always a bad –thing it can simply be a matter of interpretation.

Alongside our human psychological history there will be tips and techniques to help us change our thoughts and behaviour, to break harmful, self-perpetuating cycles. I'll look at generational shifts and the increasingly fast pace of change, all leading to some exciting, actionable takeaways for the future.

One of my favourite quotes comes from Madame de Stael, an early 19th century writer and thinker, "The human mind always makes progress, but it is a progress in spirals".

We've progressed up the spiral for thousands of years, but we're being dragged back, losing our footing, and for many it feels like we're now spiralling downwards.

We live in a world of abundance and consumption, and for many people, levels of comfort not experienced before. In the high-income countries of the world the principle of basics like shelter, food, water and comfort are not simply desired, they are expected. To arrive at this point our species has been brilliant at adaptation and the ability to endure pain and suffering in order to achieve a more comfortable way of life. Yet, in the process we've also lost something that's essential to our well-being.

So it's time to get back to the basics of human behaviour and biology – the basic functions of our species. When we understand this, we can consciously interpret and utilise our thoughts and feelings and put them to more effective use in our daily lives.

Chapter 1

Unquestionably Human

Our evolution and the core functions of human existence.

To better understand how the human mind works, we must first understand what it means to be human.

Evolution provides the best and most scientific answer when it comes to unpicking modern-day human brain function and where our thoughts, feelings and behaviours come from. So let's start by going back 70,000 years to when Homo sapiens began to advance faster and evolve more intellectually than they had done for the previous 2.5 million years.

It's important to underline that in the vast period between 2.5 million and 70,000 years ago humans were evolving from their ape relatives but at a very slow rate. The evidence suggests that throughout this vast period Homo sapiens foraged the Earth somewhere in the middle of the food chain. Evolutionary progression for humans accelerated some 70,000 years ago because this is the time experts can confidently point to when the Cognitive Revolution began with the first evidence of developed language and communication. As Homo sapiens were able to describe and discuss their world, learning was passed on faster, and our evolution began to speed up…

Let's look at just how fast our evolution moved:

70,000 years ago – The Cognitive Revolution

The first evidence of developed language and communication effectively reset the evolutionary dial for our hunter-gatherer ancestors. From here on in, things begin to speed up as small tribes start to develop skills and tools, passing on knowledge and the articulation of expertise.

12,000 years ago – The Agricultural Revolution

The domestication of plants and animals, permanent human communities and settlements are formed. Farming provides a sustainable way of life.

2,500 years ago – Creation of Coinage

Replacing a simple barter system, goods attained a more measurable value creating a currency for business and supercharging trade, which can be seen as the birth of capitalism.

2,000 years ago – Christianity and the Roman Calendar

In a dominant Roman Empire, Julius Caesar proposes a reform of the Roman calendar, including the months of July (Julius) and August (Augustus). This dating system is largely the format we continue to use today along with the use of the BCE and CE descriptors. *BC before the birth of Jesus Christ (now BCE Before*

70,000

Years Ago ← – – – – – – – – – – – – – – –

*Common Era) and AD (Anno Domini or "in the year of the Lord",
now referred to as CE Common Era) remain important markers in
human evolutionary history and dating..*

500 years ago – The Scientific Revolution

Mathematics, physics and chemistry transform humans' ability to
better understand the natural world and human biology. Advances
in medicines and energy utilisation accelerates.

200 years ago – The Industrial Revolution

The transition from hand production to mechanical methods
power our ability to mass produce goods, this industrialisation sees
humans move from the countryside to form densely populated
urban areas.

50 years ago – The Digital Revolution

The emergence of the Internet alongside innovations in computing
and mobile technology; human capability, communication and
productivity changes radically. Human life is set to be transformed.

Present Day – The Intelligence Revolution

Artificial intelligence (AI), robotics and the potential for
superintelligence along with the threat of Earth's ecological
breakdown, is set to change our world for generations to come.

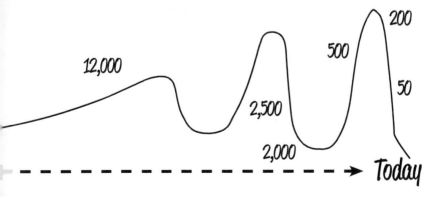

The question is,
"Will it be pain or pleasure?
Will it be for better or worse?"

So, what can we learn from history that applies helpfully to our future? How do we find a way to manage our own and humanity's many complex challenges? To stem the rising tide of anxiety and dissatisfaction? To create a more fulfilled life?

The bad news is that despite our rising levels of comfort and abundance, we seem to have lost our balance around the role of pain and pleasure in our lives: what it means, how it affects us and how to harness its power and energy.

Used by Carolus Linnaeus in 1758, the name Homo sapien comes from the Latin "wise man" and yet it seems that we're not all living up to our name.

The good news is that the answer lies in our very humanity. Because we're human, we're adaptable and (for the large part) we're incredibly intelligent.

If we are to reconnect with what it means to be human, we need to go back to the beginning, because the clues to the answers we need have been there for over 70,000 years.

At the point of the Cognitive Revolution, a hunter-gatherer's world would have looked very different to the one we live in today. Undoubtedly more dangerous, their world was, however, far simpler. In fact, they only existed and operated based on three core functions that all species on Earth share.

1. Survival
"I must stay alive!"

Self-preservation is our brain's number one innate function. Our brain needed to learn what danger looked and felt like, recognise its different forms, and move away from it. We quickly learnt to run away or hide from predators, avoid poisonous fruit, watch our footing near cliff edges and understand the danger of deep water. Every day was first and foremost about survival. Self-preservation was without question our top priority.

The brain achieved this by being both quick and effective in triggering a practical and physical response to an existential threat. Today we call this the 'fight or flight'[1] response. This response is a lightning-fast chemical change in the brain that provides an immediate hit of alertness and adrenaline, giving us a heightened focus of the mind with increased physical capacity, thus arming the mind and body to either flee or stand and fight the threat. In both cases the aim was survival, and it is the reason why still today we experience anxiety, pain and discomfort. This response needed to be uncomfortable or stressful enough for us to recognise harm or danger and therefore force us to either move away from it, or deal with it. If the fight or flight response wasn't severe enough in its level of discomfort and pain, then our hunter-gatherers wouldn't have lasted a week.

What's incredible about the brain is its ability to experience both practical and perceived pain. For hunter-gatherers this was crucial for their survival.

Practical pain and discomfort occur when we physically encounter a threat. For a hunter-gatherer this may have included burning their hand in the fire, falling on a sharp stick, or being bitten by an animal. The experience is real, the pain is physical, and it signals to the brain that it's not good for us.

Perceived pain occurs when we think that something is going to pose a threat to us. For our hunter-gatherers this was driven by memory of practical pain that they or their ancestors had encountered. In this way they quickly learnt that fire burns, certain berries poison, snakes bite and lions kill. This ability allowed them to start perceiving threats before they physically encountered them and this information gathering, and knowledge transfer was one of the main instigators for the Cognitive Revolution.

Generationally building on knowledge of their environment and the animals and plants they encountered, they increased their chances of survival through predictability and perception, together with the gradual design and use of more sophisticated tools and more consistent nutrition via the cooking, preservation and storage of food. Each generation passed on their knowledge to the younger members of the tribe and, therefore, each passing century increased the species' dominance.

No matter where we are on our time line, survival is and always will be the human brain's number one innate function. Our ability to experience practical or perceived pain and, therefore, trigger our fight or flight response, underpins our entire existence. Without it we would have become extinct almost instantly. Pain serves a hugely important purpose and, as we have evolved, this sensation has also evolved from purely a survival mechanism into a spur of motivation for many and this is something we will explore later in the book.

2. Reproduction
"I must mate and produce offspring."

After survival, reproduction and the drive for continuation is hard-wired into every species on the planet. Homo sapiens are no different and the desire to mate and provide offspring is the brain's second most innate function.

Our hunter-gatherer ancestors had a rather different philosophy to modern-day humans when it came to mating and reproduction. Between 70,000 and 35,000 years ago early hunter-gatherers existed in small tribes with a few males that did most of the mating to increase the odds of spreading their genes and, therefore, inbreeding was almost impossible to avoid. Recent research suggests[2] that around 35,000 years ago these small groups transitioned to more monogamous sexual relationships and purposely avoided the dangers of inbreeding. Interbreeding between species, Neanderthals and Homo sapiens, started to take place and by the time of the Agricultural Revolution 12,000 years ago, monogamy was pretty much established as the societal expectation for mating and reproducing. So, in the grand scheme of things, considering the vast amount of time Homo sapiens have been evolving, this relatively recent transition to monogamy suggests that we retain an element of hard-wiring around polygamous approaches to sex and reproduction. Research also suggests that Homo sapiens seeking partners beyond their immediate families in wider networks was one element that increased their chances of survival, whereas Neanderthals did not.

These small groups or tribes moved with the seasons and the availability of the plants and animals that sustained them. The groups stayed small because they were easier to feed and protect. Once offspring were born, if they were lucky enough to survive the birth, all the men in the tribe would assume collective responsibility for protecting and providing for that child. In a nutshell, it took a tribe to raise a child. If, for any reason, a mother got separated from the tribe, the chances of survival for both the lone mother and baby significantly decreased.

This hunter-gatherer approach is very different to our modern philosophy, where one male settles with one female in a formalised partnership to raise their own offspring until adulthood. This has given rise to a theory around modern-day infidelity in which some psychologists suggest our ancestors' approach to mating and nurturing means humans were not meant to mate for life with one person; our species did not evolve by males and females being in only one long-term sexual relationship. Evolution, one could argue, has hard-wired the human brain to be rewarded for seeking out and mating with as many of the opposite sex as possible. It's why the pleasure of sexual intercourse is so rewarding: there must be a desire, a drive and a reward great enough for us to prioritise this task and thus ensure the continuation of the species.

Just as survival is the number one driver for moving away from pain, sexual intercourse is the number one driver for seeking pleasure.

Darwin's theory of evolution by natural selection revolutionised the way we understand our species and these behaviours. In 1859, Charles Darwin set out his theory as an explanation for adaptation (how genes passed on to offspring enabled physical or behavioural adaptation that helped organisms better survive in their environment) and speciation (when a group within a species separates away and develops unique characteristics)[3]. Darwin defined natural selection as the *"principle by which each slight variation* [of a trait], *if useful, is preserved"*. if you put this into the context of early Homo sapiens, then we can conclude that females would look for the strongest and most admirable traits in the males and actively seek out mating with them in order to give their offspring the greatest chance of survival. Males, on the other hand, would simply seek to sow their seed with as many females as possible to continue their lineage. This is why males would fight and compete to become the alpha or leader, as it would result in priority of mating rights with the females.

Today, reproduction and the continuation of our species remains one of our three core functions. We may approach it differently, in terms of the way we go about it, but ultimately, the primal instinct of seeking out a desirable partner, mating with them and nurturing our offspring to adulthood is as important, daunting and rewarding today, as it was 100,000 years ago. Reproduction is the core reason why the pleasure system of our mind and body exists, to encourage and reward mating. Just as a threat triggers the pain response to alert us for survival, attraction and desire trigger the pleasure response for sex.

From the earliest evolution of humans, pain and pleasure sensations in the body and mind motivated and governed all our thoughts, actions and behaviours. To keep us alive and continue our species. No matter how much more sophisticated you believe us to be today, this remains the case.

The Survival/Reproduction Interplay – *What's interesting about our first two innate functions is the interplay between them. Once reproduction has taken place and our offspring are born, our survival instinct heightens, becoming more active and potent. Our awareness of danger and sensitivity to perceived risk significantly increases because, as parents or caregivers, we now carry the burden of survival, not just for ourselves, but also on behalf of our offspring until they reach adulthood and possess the ability to protect and provide for themselves.*

For our hunter-gatherers this presented a very uncertain time for the tribe as they moved, hunted, foraged and sought shelter; difficult at the best of times, imagine doing it whilst carrying two or three babies, plus a toddler in tow. The same applies in modern-day life. If you have ever wondered why your levels of anxiety have significantly increased after becoming a parent, this evolutionary explanation will give you the answer. No, you're not going crazy; you're not weak or inadequate, you are experiencing the biological effects of reproduction and parenthood. You are carrying the burden of survival on behalf of your children. You are simply being human.

3. Purpose
"I must contribute to the tribe."

The brain's third and final core function is purpose. Following closely behind self-preservation, providing offspring and looking after the tribe, our hunter-gatherer ancestors also ordered themselves within their tribes based on roles and contribution. Although it would have been very simple and limited to the same handful of roles, it was important that a hierarchy and sense of contribution was formed for the tribe to be successful. For example, there would almost certainly be a leader, this would have been what's often described as an alpha male. There would have been the foragers, the hunters and the caregivers. Yes, all members of a hunter-gatherer tribe would have the responsibility to do all these things if required, but, as the tribe increased, some would possess greater abilities and skills in certain areas and therefore the tribe would naturally organise itself into roles.

These roles would also give each tribe member a value to the leader and therefore, most crucially for them, acceptance and protection by both him and the tribe. This represents the first origins of individual purpose and is also very important in terms of understanding how our modern-day psychology works.

Today, we are no different. Yes, we need to survive and ensure the continuation of our species and I think we have pretty much cracked this, as so many live in a world of relative comfort and safety. In which case I believe it is purpose that is arguably the most important and impactful core function of our modern existence. Sex may give us periodic and fleeting moments of pleasure, but it is purpose that ultimately shapes our experiences and delivers fulfilment at a much deeper level and in a more meaningful way. However, establishing a real sense of purpose today is much more complex and multi-faceted than it was for our forebears.

Modern-day humans are suffering from what I call 'role overload'.

Here at T2, we have accumulated thousands of data points and a large body of research on humans and their motivation, behaviour and, ultimately, their purpose. When we conduct 1-2-1 interviews and coaching sessions, we always try to unearth what drives a person's sense of purpose:

- **What motivates them?**

- **How do they feel they contribute to society or in life?**

- **What are they striving to achieve?**

- **What brings them happiness and a sense of a fulfilment?**

Our research tells us that purpose is difficult to define for many modern-day humans. There are many reasons for this but, primarily, I believe it's because of role overload. So, let's look deeper into role overload: and the possible roles of hunter-gatherers versus modern humans...

If you look at the examples listed below, and I'm sure there's more we could add to the modern-day human list, you can see that over a period of around 100,000 years the roles of an average human have increased fourfold. At first glance, this may appear that it should give us four times more purpose than our ancestors ever had, right? However, our findings suggest that the management and prioritisation of multiple roles, along with our effectiveness in fulfilling them, can be both diluting and overwhelming, leading to feelings of burden and failure, as opposed to fulfilment and success.

Modern-day Human Roles

Father/Mother
Husband/Wife
Son/Daughter
Sibling
Cousin
Nephew/Niece
Uncle/Aunt
Grandparent
Friend

Hunter-gatherer Roles

Mate
Protector
Provider
Caregiver

Entrepreneur
Career Professional
Leader
Colleague
Sports Coach
Volunteer
Hobbyist

Now, combine this role overload with information overload, representing the number of inputs we receive into the brain on an average day. A modern-day human receives more information inputs in a single day than our hunter-gatherers did in their entire lifetime! Let that sink in. The science and numbers behind it are staggering and this combined overload can lead to a distorted sense of self, purpose and contribution. It seems we are dealing with an overwhelming abundance of information and responsibility that can leave many staggering, if not crushed under the weight of personal and societal expectation and we will be exploring this later in the book.

Another very interesting statistic has emerged from our ongoing research about human need and purpose and reinforces our core functions. Over one-third of all respondents across 16,000 assessments stated that their number one need was **to live in an orderly world, without chaos** and the second was **to serve other human beings, have connection and care for others**.

Let's think back to our hunter-gatherer tribe that offered security, protection and connection. Over a gap of thousands of years, we have compelling evidence that we humans still seek the same things, yet, even with our vastly expanded resources and comfort, we are still struggling to find purpose and contentment.

So, we know that purpose, our third core function of human existence, enables us to connect with, and better understand, how we fit into society and contribute to the world around us. Fundamentally, it gives us our sense of belonging, helps us understand how we contribute and validates how we make a difference.

In Charles Darwin's book, *On the Origin of Species* (1859), he states, *"Homo sapiens are just another kind of animal"*. On publication this notion was met with outrage: people believed that Homo sapiens had clear, different and distinctive cognitive capabilities compared to all other species on Earth, mainly our ability to innovate and problem solve through the perception of foresight, our imagination and our ability to invent fiction. Importantly, Darwin was pointing out that on a primal, core functional level, we, along with all living species, are governed by the same three things: survival, reproduction and purpose. Natural Selection was the theory that reasoned evolution relied on these three core functions to pass on a species' most desirable genes and traits to offspring in order to ensure the most advantageous and continuous progression coining the phrases "Survival of the fittest" and "Only the strong survive".

Remember, too, Darwin's theory around adaptation? How genes passed down to the next generation allow species to adapt better physically and behaviourally to their future environment? Meaning that although we continue to adapt, our core functions will always remain the same; without them we would become extinct. For example, survival is still as important today as it was 70,000 years ago, however, the adaptation is that we now no longer need to outrun a predator or climb a tree, and therefore we don't need the physical fitness or prowess we once possessed. Instead, we need higher cognitive functioning to problem solve and work out things like the logistics and provision of energy and foods. The same core function of survival is the driver, however, it's the modern-day human brain and body that has adapted from those that existed thousands of years ago.

Our species has spent 100,000 years evolving with increasing rapidity. Our cognitive capabilities, intellect and knowledge have significantly increased. Our world has become more advanced, and we have transformed the way modern-day humans live. However, despite all these advantages, we can scientifically and confidently conclude that the mechanisms and origins of all human thoughts, feelings, behaviours and actions are hard-wired in our brains through evolution. We, as a species, remain unequivocally motivated towards pleasure (reproduction and purpose) and away from pain (survival).

But, is our evolutionary hard-wiring, once our biggest asset, today our greatest challenge?

We no longer run from wild animals or risk our lives every time we leave the tribe. No longer do we die from poisoning, very rarely do we fall to our death, and we have significantly reduced our chances of dying from illness and disease with the improvements in our healthcare, medicines and vaccinations. Yet despite this and our increasing levels of comfort and safety, the evidence points to the fact that for many, our lives do not give us the pleasure or fulfilment they once did.

This begs the question, how do our core functions of survival, reproduction and purpose work for us in 2024 and beyond? How does our brain's ability to experience and perceive pain and pleasure influence our thoughts, decisions and actions in our modern world? Most importantly, is this serving us well? If not, how do we tip the balance back in our favour?

To be able to start answering these questions and begin our journey back to balance, let's now focus on pain and pleasure and how, despite our highly sophisticated world, we are still ruled by these powerful instincts and sensations.

Onward we go...

Chapter 2

Pain and Pleasure

Everything we do is governed by either pain or pleasure.

Now that we have navigated the last 70,000 years of human evolution and established that all human thoughts, actions and behaviours are motivated by our need to endure pain or experience pleasure, let's take a closer look at what pain and pleasure mean for us.

The Pain-Pleasure Complex: a complex system of mind and body that forms the main motivation behind all our thoughts, beliefs, actions and behaviours.

Pain is both a mental and physical sensation: it feels uncomfortable, challenging or painful and leads us to move away from or avoid whatever gives us these sensations.

Pleasure is both a mental and physical sensation: a feeling of comfort, contentment and reward, which leads us to seek and repeat whatever gives us these sensations.

The pain-pleasure complex, however, is not straightforward. It is perhaps best understood, when we consider that we are hard-wired to adopt the preference of avoiding pain and seeking pleasure in almost all situations apart from two.

The first is that which gives us a greater reward in exchange for some pain; this can be seen as developmental or growth.

The second is that where true survival is at stake, we must take action to confront or avoid the threat causing us pain; we stand and fight or we take flight.

The three psychological states of the Pain-Pleasure Complex

Given what we now know about the pain-pleasure complex, we humans can be in one of three psychological states at any one time:

 1. Neutral State – in this state we avoid pain, seek comfort and our motivation is towards pleasure and contentment. We are in our comfort zone. At home with our feet up watching a movie, pottering in the garden, snoozing on the sofa or taking a gentle walk. Neither stressed nor elated. We are at 'rest' and experiencing recovery.

 2. Challenge State – in this state we seek pleasure and reward, yet to do so will involve us enduring some pain. Our motivation is towards pleasure through reward and fulfilment. We are out of our comfort zone, we may be taking on a complex role at work, moving house or even writing a book. Experiencing stress, experiencing risk and feeling challenged, but all in a bid to achieve a goal or outcome

 3. Threat State – in this state we seek to avoid an immediate or perceived threat and our motivation is purely to survive. We may be balancing on a high ledge, public speaking, accused of something, in deep water or receiving unexpected news from the GP, all of which can plunge us into Threat State.

Throughout the history of human evolution we have survived primarily because we possessed the ability to balance these three states and interchange between them effectively. Not because we wanted to but because we had to.

Our ability to balance the pain-pleasure scales enables us to make space for our **Neutral State**, giving us crucial time for rest, relaxation and recovery, so that we can push into periods of **Challenge State**, which is required to take risks, at the same time understanding that we would occasionally have to face up to and deal with **Threat State** situations, should we encounter something that posed a serious threat to us or our tribe. This 'balance' has seen us flourish for many years with each state proving highly effective for achieving survival, reproduction and purpose.

> *Our hunter-gatherer ancestors would have got up in the morning in Neutral State, but would then have to move into a Challenge State to hunt for food. If successful there was a reward, meaning they could move back into Neutral State. If they didn't find or catch anything for the hungry tribe the Challenge State would persist, and more effort would be made to find food. A predator on the horizon may have taken it up a notch to Threat State. When that was dealt with and food found, back at the campsite the tribe would return to a Neutral State as the day drew to an end. Being able to switch up and push into different states of being and having the resilience and motivation to go through challenges, is just as important as the ability to switch into the Neutral State, to reset and recharge ready for the next day.*

To better understand how these three states are induced, and our ability to switch between them, we need to look more closely at the way our brains interpret and signal pain and pleasure. First on the list is dopamine.

Dopamine is a neuromodulator, a molecule that is stored in the brain that acts as a neurotransmitter. Think of it as an organic chemical that, when released into the brain, gives us the desire and motivation to act. In popular culture and the modern media, dopamine is often portrayed as the main chemical of pleasure, but recent pharmacological and psychological research suggests that dopamine is, more accurately, the main chemical for motivation along with movement and memory. In other words, dopamine signals or instigates the motivation around a perceived outcome, which in turn drives our behaviour towards or away from it.

People assume that motivation is purely associated with pleasure and achievement, when really it is equally about the avoidance of pain. Motivation is simply the driving force behind our need to survive, reproduce and have purpose.

We now understand that a dopamine release in our brain is controlled by the anticipation of a reward or outcome, so that we will put in the work and commitment required to achieve it rather than the actual result itself. Dopamine is the starting gun, its release on our circuits and cells is essentially saying, "The conditions are good. The opportunity is worth it. Despite the risk, challenge or pain, let's go for it!"

And because it is the anticipation of reward that causes dopamine release, and not the result of our actions, this explains why we are willing to take on challenging endeavours. If the vision and purpose behind an action are strong, our dopamine release causes a surge in our motivation to work hard, accept the difficulties and endure the challenge.

Once the goal has been achieved and the rewards enjoyed, our dopamine levels very quickly return to, or even drop below, their baseline level. This manifests as a post elation 'slump'. Reflect on your own life for a moment and think about when you achieved something significant. You may have delivered a presentation, launched or completed a project, moved house, won a race or returned from an amazing holiday. The feelings of anti-climax and lethargy you experience once it's over are the physical signs of dopamine depletion.

If the reward is not achieved despite our hard work, and yet we continue to persevere, our dopamine release can be twice as strong in anticipation of eventually achieving our goal. So those who fail at first and then again and again, but through perseverance eventually achieve their goal, experience much greater satisfaction and reward. Those who give up on their endeavours, however, can cause the opposite effect in the form of demotivation, as a negative psychological anchor is planted, which in turn reduces their perceived level of competence and confidence.

Another thing that's important to know about the ability of the brain to produce and store dopamine is that following a dopamine releasing encounter or event, it takes time for our dopamine to fully restore to its baseline levels. This results in us being in a temporary negative or depleted state.

Scientists don't exactly know the timing from human to human of how quickly we replenish dopamine. But what we do know is that it's not instant, and because we are all unique, it stands to reason that our recovery times will all differ. So, the ability to recover in our Neutral State is essential for our well-being; we need to rest, reset and be ready for our next challenge or threat. We cannot seek dopamine releasing events continuously for this reason.

A greater understanding of how dopamine operates within the brain means that we can also get a better understanding of how addiction works. For example, if you continually and rapidly engage in encounters and events that trigger the release of dopamine, then, sooner or later, your overall dopamine levels are going to be diminished to the point at which you can no longer receive the same amount of elation or pleasure from repeating that activity. This means you need to take it up a notch to regain that sensory feeling or seek greater pleasure elsewhere. Experiencing daily micro rushes of dopamine can also lead to depletion and an inability to fully replenish baseline levels.

In her book, *Dopamine Nation*, Dr Anna Lembke[4] articulately explains why today we are suffering the effects of diminished dopamine brought about by the high levels of daily activities that trigger its release. Dr Lembke also explores the science behind addiction and how dopamine works in retrospect with addictive behaviours. And it's not just about addictive drugs and substances; Dr Lembke comments:

> *"The world now offers a full complement of digital drugs that didn't exist before, or if they did exist, they now exist on digital platforms that have exponentially increased their potency and availability. These include online pornography, gambling and video games, to name a few."*

Dr Lembke is referring to the highly accessible and addictive online activities that are built to engage and encourage us to repeat an activity again and again. It's worth pausing for a moment to consider the effect on the younger generation growing up today, a generation with greater access and exposure to more sexualised, violent and addictive online content than ever before. A reduction in our ability to replenish and store baseline dopamine levels, combined with our inability to experience pleasure due to repeated exposure and the subsequent mind-numbing effects, could, it's argued, inhibit normal sexual relationships and encounters. One of the human brain's core functions becoming overwhelmed and short circuited.

The technology we use to access these 'digital drugs' in the form of smart TVs, computers, tablets and phones are also highly addictive in themselves. The lights, notifications, chat sounds and anticipation of updates have a significant impact on our brain function as they create a perpetual cycle of dopamine release time after time.

"Finally, on June 29, 2007, boredom was pronounced dead, thanks to the iPhone. And so our imaginations and deep social connections went with it." Michael Easter[5]

How many of us lose track of time to the 'pull to refresh' action on every social media app, an easy to repeat, highly addictive universal action that delivers an unending scroll of seemingly happy and high-flying lifestyles? Very rarely do we share our pain and insecurities on social media. This can lead to a distorted belief around our own lives. Why do I have troubles and others don't? Why am I not running down the beach with my family? Why don't I get a new car every 12 months, or look good in a bikini? The reality is that we all suffer, we all have challenges, because we are all human. Highly curated, carefully selected and often filtered social media posts can feed our insecurities and form a narrative that we are alone in our struggle. Whereas nothing could be further than the truth.

Let's check back in with our hunter-gatherers and how dopamine would have affected their daily lives versus us modern-day Homo sapiens. A hunter-gatherer's brain would release dopamine motivating them to take on encounters and events that constituted survival, reproduction and purpose only. It was a simple formula that kicked in a handful of times a day around finding food, keeping the tribe safe or maybe to mate and provide offspring. It was the brain's way of mobilising and motivating them to fulfil the three basic functions of human existence and to secure the continuation of the species. Now fast forward to a modern-day human brain.

Dopamine release has gone into overdrive with multiple bursts based on short-term immediate gratification gains and rewards. This creates a whole new cycle of dopamine production, uptake and release that the brain cannot keep up with. A consequence is that we are potentially operating within a continuous state of dopamine depletion, gradually reducing our ability to achieve pleasure in normal and natural everyday encounters and events. We must then overcompensate in a bid to experience pleasure and reward, further exacerbating the problem.

Consumption and pleasure – a cautionary tale

Some years ago my brother and I, together with our families, were lucky enough to take a joint holiday in Mexico staying at the Moon Palace Resort. It was the most amazing resort we had ever been to. Everything was five star – the accommodation, the service, the food, the beach, everything was out of this world. We boldly claimed at the time, and often still do, that there is no better place in the world to go on holiday. This is probably the worst thing we could have done. Since then we have both been on some amazing holidays but on our return, we always seem to have the same conversation:

"How was it?"

"Yeah, it was good, but it was no Moon Palace."

"Yes but, nothing ever will be…"

Now when we were growing up, my brother and I only had one overseas holiday. We travelled to the South of France in the back of an old Ford Orion with no air conditioning and we lived in a tent for two weeks. I remember it as being amazing. Yet, today, it feels like we and our families have access to so many luxury opportunities and trips that we experience diminishing returns of pleasure and reward from them. The reality is that it shouldn't matter where we go or how luxurious it is, we should enjoy the time spent with family and soak up the sun, the company, and enjoy a well-earned period in our Neutral State. But this is what happens in the brain when you combine repetitive exposure and grandiose consumption around a single activity, event or experience.

Ultimately, accessibility and consumption are creating a Low Road versus High Road dilemma for our brains' reward systems.

The High, Low Road Dilemma

Our brains have evolved to be very good at assessing situations and applying an unconscious scale of motivation against them. To articulate this scale simply, I call it Low Road versus High Road motivation.

Low Road Motivation – short-term quick or immediate relief, results, gains or gratification.

High Road Motivation – long-term delayed relief, results, gains or gratification.

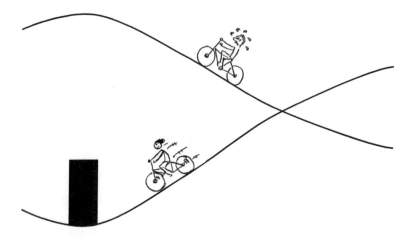

The Low Road describes a situation or activity that gives quick or immediate relief, results, gains or gratification; you will get an instant reward and the effort and commitment is likely to be minimal or easily achievable.

The High Road describes a situation or activity that offers delayed relief, results, gains or gratification; you will not necessarily see quick rewards and it's likely to involve personal sacrifice, effort and commitment over a longer period in order to achieve the goal. It may also carry some risk.

A good example of comparing a Low Road to High Road motivation would be wanting to make a change to our health and fitness.

Going to the gym is a High Road motivation scenario, whereas ordering some weight-loss pills and an abs machine from the Internet is a Low Road motivation scenario. It's going to take three to six months before we see results from our efforts in the gym, committing at least five to six hours a week, alongside the aches, pains and fatigue that training inevitably brings with it, plus our more disciplined, healthier eating habits.

Now, going to the gym for three to six months, plus the commitment, sacrifice and dedication required will, without question, deliver the results we want – it could change our lives, BUT ... today, we live in a world where the Low Road motivation alternatives are both easily accessible and desirable. A quick search on the Internet and £100 later we have a bottle of weight-loss pills and an abs machine arriving on our doorstep within 24 hours. The Low Road wins, only for us to abandon the ineffective pills and ill-fitting machine within two weeks, as we discover that neither have any effect.

The dilemma we all face in modern-day life is choosing High Road situations and alternatives over the temptation for continuous and readily available Low Road options. What Anne Lambke's *Dopamine Nation* and Michael Easter's *The Comfort Crisis* both identify is an increasing imbalance in our motivation. Compared to hunter-gatherers who had no choice in the matter, the world we live in today offers many more Low Road options than ever before, leading us to form habits around instant gratification and reduced effort. For example, a hunter-gatherer going out to hunt and forage would constitute High Road motivation. Why? Because it represented an arduous, dangerous and sometimes fruitless endeavour. The reward wasn't guaranteed, never mind delayed. However, they had the motivation of survival to propel them into action every day. Consider that compared to many modern-day humans who don't even have to move from the sofa to order their 'catch of the day' and receive it within 30 minutes on their doorstep, even though they already have two cupboards filled with food and all they need to do is walk to the kitchen to get it.

Low effort equals instant results

Another example is around social connection and meaningful interactions. Before the creation of the Internet, and before that the telephone, there was a time 30 to 50 years ago when we had to put in effort to engage with others and make friends. We had to go out, connect with other people and build rapport in order to find common ground and receive the reward of friendship and companionship. Today we only need to post a photograph or a statement on social media to receive instant likes, comments and validation. Or we can register on a dating website to view potential people we like the look of to arrange a date or engage in flirty behaviour. Again, low effort equals instant results.

The easier something is and the quicker the reward, the more likely we are going to become addicted to or repeat that pattern of behaviour. And as we have already explored, the more frequently we engage in that activity, the less likely we are to receive pleasure from it. We quickly become numb to its effects. So we need to up the stakes. We either double or triple down on the activity or we push the envelope to find something more rewarding that's equally as quick and hard hitting. Simultaneously, this reduces our resilience when it comes to the arduous, challenging and delayed gratification of the High Road because we now possess the ability to easily avoid it. The quick and easy rewards of the Low Road are gradually eroding our ability to even sense the meaning behind a more difficult, yet ultimately more rewarding alternative.

This erosion of mental resilience is significantly distorting and inhibiting our ability to experience pleasure and endure pain in a balanced and productive way. The scales have tipped. Our entire motivation system is being hijacked; no longer in balance, no longer keeping us fighting fit for both low and high motivation, turning us into Low Road motivation machines. Reflect for a moment on a time in your life, when, faced with a decision around Low and High Road motivations, you opted for the easier route of instant gratification and reward. There are likely to be many, aren't there?

Let's just remind ourselves about our Neutral, Challenge and Threat States:

Neutral State: Avoid pain. Seek comfort. Motivation towards pleasure. Contentment and comfort.

Challenge State: Seek Pleasure. Endure pain. Motivation towards pleasure. Reward and fulfilment.

Threat State: Avoid immediate threat or pain. Motivation away from pain. Fight or flight.

Low Road motivation seems to perpetually want to put us in a Neutral State; our comfort zone, the state of rest, relaxation and ease in which we will experience little challenge and pain in exchange for contentment and comfort. I think one of the best fictional depictions of this state is the 2008 Pixar movie *Wall-E*. After mass ecological breakdown on Earth, all the surviving humans live on a spaceship. They recline on floating comfy chairs and everything on board is designed for their ease and comfort. From eating and moving around to activities and relationships. So much so that they've lost the ability to stand up, walk or think for themselves. The writers are taking aspects of our current way of life and evolving it to the point of a never-ending Neutral State underpinned by Low Road motivation. At first it appears so calm and comfortable, but it's empty. Ultimately, the film's narrative takes them to a joyous return to Earth, helped by plucky robots, to re-establish a better, more fulfilling and sustainable way of life. We need to ask ourselves is this what we want for our future? A life based on continuous Low Road motivation with every comfort catered for, yet devoid of challenge?

It is our ability but also our need to seek out situations, events and activities that thrust us into both Challenge and Threat States that will push us to take on High Road motivation activities. This will ultimately condition us to endure the suffering and pain required to increase our resilience threshold. Yes, the Neutral State plays a key role. After all, it's very effective in allowing us to replenish our baseline dopamine levels. It helps us recharge and reset our systems ready to go again because it is impossible to be in Challenge or Threat States or High Road motivation situations all the time. We are not primed for this either. Even our hunter-gatherer ancestors found solace in relaxing around the campfire or engaging in play with their children. The key lies in our ability to balance our states and manage our motivation appropriately. We must, as humans, get back to finding time and space for our Neutral State, whilst also finding meaningful and intermittent situations that thrust us into Challenge State, which builds our knowledge and strengthens our ability to deal with Threat State situations as they arise. This balance will allow us to get back to a more intermittent pain and pleasure approach, and this we will explore in more detail later in the book.

The Origins of Pain and Pleasure

Now that we have established our need to balance pain and pleasure, let's look at how the mind and body enables us to experience them in the first place. There are two organs full of nerves, neurons, cells and receptors that are designed to identify, or experience, pain and pleasure. These organs are the skin and the brain.

Our skin

Full of nerves, neurons and cells, our skin can pick up pain and pleasure by touch (pressure and trauma) or by temperature (hot and cold). This is a reactive physical response to pain or pleasure.

Our skin and pain

Hunter-gatherers quickly learnt about pain through the nerves and neurons in their skin having harmful and troubling encounters. Pressure and blunt force trauma to the body would be instantly registered by the brain, but the signal would originate from the skin, as would encounters with hot or cold substances like ice, fire and scorching sunlight. The skin plays a crucial role in our ability to experience physical pain.

Our skin and pleasure

Just as our skin triggers signals of pain through pressure or trauma, it also can signal pleasure through sensitive or sexual stimulation. Leading neuroscientist and ophthalmologist Andrew Huberman[6] and his team perform 3D mapping of the human brain, giving them a full picture of the human nervous system, including the corresponding neurons, nerves and cells for each area of the body. Huberman's research has shown that the lips, genitals and fingertips consist of many more cells, nerves and neurons than any other part of the body, meaning that they are the most perceptive and sensitive areas for experiencing pain and pleasure by touch. This explains why, when you take a sip of hot coffee it feels excruciating, or when you pick up a hot pan you drop it instantly. It's also why we find things like tickling, scratching, massage therapy or mating activities like kissing and sexual intercourse highly pleasurable.

Just as our skin plays a vital role in our survival, it also plays a role in one of our other core functions: reproduction. Our skin's ability to create pleasant sensations in both our mind and body encourages us to engage in activities that fulfil the need to continue our species.

Quick sensitivity test: to understand how sensitive your skin is, try this easy test. Take two relatively sharp pencils. Hold them in one hand side by side. Now gently push both points against your lower lip. How many points of contact to you feel? Now do the same action but on the top of your bare arm. How many clear points of contact do you feel now? You should have felt two points of contact on your lip, clearly indicating two pencils whereas, on your upper arm, you should have felt one point of contact, indicating only one pencil. This disparity is because your lips have many more cells, nerves and neurons than your arm.

Our brains

Full of nerves, neurons and cells that register pain and pleasure through sight, prediction and perception, or as a direct result of the physical sensations in the skin.

Our brain and pain

The brain's ability to predict pain is necessary both for our survival and our ability to assess pain and pleasure accurately. Back to Andrew Huberman again. Huberman and his team have identified that it's the timing of the prediction that matters. If the prediction happens well in advance of the painful event, it makes the pain worse. If the prediction happens a few seconds before the event, giving us no time to prepare, again it makes the effect of the pain worse. However, if the prediction of pain happens around a minute before the event, mental and physical preparation can reduce the pain. The brain's ability to predict an outcome is designed for us to spot potential pain coming our way, allowing us to be mentally and physically prepared and thus reducing its effects in our minds.

So, the brain's prediction of pain, either well in advance or seconds before, is suboptimal, giving space for anxiety and shock to come into play. This ability to predict potential pain or danger is subjective from human to human, as is the ability to experience pleasure. It's worth noting that no one reading this book will have the same experiences or view the world in the same way.

Our sight

Vision also plays a key role in the brain's ability to predict pain or danger. There are two types of vision: sight and imagination. Sight is what we see before us in the real world, although there can still be an element of perception associated with this. In the main, however, it will be a true representation of what is happening in the here and now. Imagination is what we foresee or what could happen in the future, which is built entirely on prediction and perception of future events. And it is this, our imagination, that is the cause of most occurrences of Threat State in modern-day life.

Hypothetical worrying is often the number one cause of anxiety in the people I coach. After a few questions, it's very clear that the person in front of me is experiencing a Threat State due to hypothetical anxiety: their fear of something that hasn't happened yet. This is imagination at work, and it plays an important role in our core survival function.

The ability to predict danger and pain has kept us alive for hundreds of thousands of years. Today, however, it appears that we are struggling to differentiate between true and perceived threats, which has seen hypothetical worrying become a common problem for many modern-day humans.

Our brain and pleasure

The brain's ability to experience pleasure exists to serve both our core functions of reproduction and purpose. Our old friend dopamine together with serotonin and oxytocin play a large role in our ability to experience pleasure in a whole range of different situations. Dopamine, as we've explored, supports our motivation to act; oxytocin, however, is regarded as our bonding chemical. It is released when we feel connection, trust and rapport with other humans and plays a vital role in a mother's instant bond with a baby. Oxytocin also plays a role in our social connections and friendships. If you have ever said, "I love you!" to someone (and meant it) it's probably the oxytocin talking.

Serotonin, amongst other things, is a brain chemical that helps us to feel significant or important and plays a role in supporting our purpose, giving us the feeling that we are making a difference to someone or something.

Pleasure is, by and large, associated with comfort, safety, relaxation and relationships when we are in our Neutral State. However, it also has important associations with purpose, achievement and triumph associated with the Challenge State. The one time you are unlikely to experience pleasure is if you are in the middle of a Threat State situation. This is because a brain chemical called cortisol is released that triggers our fight or flight response. Cortisol gives us that spine-tingling, hair-raising sense of immediate danger, uncertainty or anxiety and is usually accompanied by a shot of adrenaline, which primes our body's physical readiness to deal with the threat.

Cortisol and adrenaline are the reasons why, if you have ever put yourself in a Threat State-inducing situation like a bungee jump, a skydive or even just something like speaking in public, the details in the aftermath are sketchy. You can't seem to recall every moment of what happened. This is often the effect of the cortisol and adrenaline pumping through your system. They have very specific tasks, which don't include perfect recall. Their job is to increase your heart rate, tunnel your vision, reduce your fine motor skills and pump blood to your muscles. It doesn't feel remotely comfortable, but by the time you hit the ground following your skydive you are flooded with serotonin and dopamine along with feelings of relief, achievement and elation as the Threat State subsides a feeling no amount of likes or comments on Facebook can ever match! Now THAT is the value of High Road motivation.

Losing our balance...

An integral system of our mind and body, we've explored the pain and pleasure complex, which is the motivation behind all our thoughts, beliefs, actions and behaviours primarily underpinning our evolutionary core functions of survival, reproduction and purpose.

Pain and pleasure are experienced through our senses and organs: our skin, vision and brain function, including our imagination.

Dopamine plays a huge role in our motivation towards pleasure or away from pain. This leads us to be in one of three states at any one time: Neutral, Challenge or Threat.

The inability to balance our motivation around pain and pleasure is causing modern-day humans greater challenges, as an abundance of resource and immediacy of gratification is leading us down a path of repetitive patterns of Low Road motivation as we seek perpetual comfort, pleasure and reward. This pattern is creating a change in our dopamine production and uptake capacity, inhibiting our ability to engage in High Road motivation events and activities. Given all this, we can now start to see how and why we're losing our balance.

So where does this leave us?

Although we are all part of the same species, and have the same evolutionary traits, we are all unique and have very different experiences of life. Is our balance further unsettled by our individual nature and nurturing? What role do these important forces play in forging our susceptibility to Low or High Road motivation? And, despite our primal evolutionary drivers and dopamine-sapping modern lives, can we change tack and get better at finding our balance?

Well, that's where we're heading next. I'm going to take a deep dive into the powerful forces that forge and mould our childhood and early adolescent brains. By unlocking the clues in our early life we can start to understand the behaviours and patterns we continue to use as adults. Let's now explore the inner workings of you!

Chapter 3

Nature and Nurture

Exploring the elements that forge our personality.

Up to this point we have explored the history of Homo sapiens and identified our basic functions, common needs and the desires we all share as a species. This, however, is not the whole picture.

Current psychology and behavioural science tell us that, although we are all primarily governed by and motivated towards pleasure or away from pain, underpinned by our core functions of survival, reproduction and purpose, HOW each of us individually respond to these motivations dramatically differs. This variance is due to our different personality styles and cognitive programming, and these are the result of the unique combination and interplay between our nature and our nurture.

Our nature is governed by the biochemistry we have inherited: the mix of genes from our mothers and fathers.

Our nurture is developed by our cognitive programming through exposure to our environment: our external experiences and influences mainly, parental, social and educational.

On average our brains become fully developed by the time we are 23 to 26 years old, although for some this can be up to 30 years old. By this stage we will have also developed our distinctive personality type formed by our behavioural and social preferences, combined with our view of the world: how we think the world should work and how we fit in.

So, let's now dive a little deeper into the concepts of Nature and Nurture, and help you to start building a picture of your own unique self and make some interesting discoveries along the way.

Human Nature

The blueprint of our biochemistry.

When a child is conceived, they inherit 50% of their father's genes and 50% of their mother's. Siblings (except identical twins) will not, however, inherit the same 50% split. By and large, you and your siblings get around 50% of the same genes and 50% that are different.

Think about it this way: if each parent's genes were represented by a deck of 52 cards, you would receive 26 cards from each parent's deck. Any sibling would also receive 26 cards from each parent, but they will not be the same 26 cards and, therefore, while their genetic make-up will share some similarities with you, the overall make-up of their DNA will differ.

The 'family footprint'

Our inherited genes determine some obvious things such as, skin colour, eye colour, hair colour, height, body type and blood group. They also, more interestingly perhaps, give us genetic dispositions to certain behavioural characteristics. This means that even though we all share our species' evolutionary biology and three core functions of human existence, once born we are already 50% on our way to forming our own unique personality type and world view based purely on the genetics of our parents, setting us on a course without any environmental influences at all.

Our minds under a microscope

As we explore Nature and Nurture it's worth differentiating and defining the two main influences in the world of behavioural science and neurobiology.

Neurobiologists, *or Neuroscientists, focus on the biochemistry, anatomy and molecular biology of our nervous systems, including the neurons, circuits and cells in the brain, spinal cord and nerves. They conduct experiments to explore our physical make-up, including brain imaging, cell and tissue microscopy, and genetic analysis.*

Psychologists *focus on our mental processing. They explore how our minds produce thoughts, beliefs and behaviours. Their work involves experimentation and studies through observation and interpretation of how we individually relate and respond to each other and our environment.*

Neurobiologists largely believe that our genetics and biochemistry dictate our natural predisposition for experiencing pain and pleasure. They believe its mainly governed by our Nature.

Although they do acknowledge that environmental, psychological and sociological factors may shape it throughout our lives, they believe it to be predominantly influenced by our genetic make-up.

Think of it like a personal genetic scale numbered 1–10, with 10 being euphoric and 1 being utterly depressed. The hypothesis is that our genes preset a range on that scale for us, say between 4 and 7, from the moment we're born, and our experience of pleasure and happiness simply moves between those points, no lower, no higher.

Any alteration to that preset scale, in the case of supporting someone experiencing medically diagnosed low mood or long-term depression, for example, would need drugs to chemically manipulate their biochemistry. This intervention would seek to enhance serotonin uptake or dopamine production to shift the needle higher up the scale and enable that person to benefit from improved mood and contentment.

 Psychologists, on the other hand, observe and interpret human behaviour through questioning an individual and scoring, reviewing and processing the information captured. This leads to identifying patterns of behaviour and building a picture of behavioural tendencies relating to someone's environment and those around them. Many psychologists believe that our ability to experience pain and pleasure is largely triggered by our environment, relationships and circumstances. They believe it is mainly governed by Nurture. Psychologists support individuals through talking and/or behavioural therapy.

A note here on the role of psychiatrists. Psychiatrists are medical doctors. They diagnose illness, prescribe drugs and manage treatment for complex mental illness, drawing on both neurobiology and psychology.

Both neurobiologists and psychologists present compelling arguments, however they both agree that it is our ability to balance the pain-pleasure complex that helps us live our best lives over a sustained period.

We need our pain and pleasure in balance to support the longevity of our mental and physical well-being.

Having explored Nature and the preset of our genetic coding, lets now look at the other half of our make-up, the environmental influences that shape our Nurture.

Human Nurture

How the external world shapes our identity.

So, you're around two or three years old and to this point your brain has been working really hard on forming and connecting the synapses required to learn the basics of survival: recognising caregivers; drinking and eating; gripping objects and picking things up; attracting attention by babbling, crying and learning speech; and moving by crawling and climbing, effectively mastering the early cognitive abilities and fine motor skills required to grow, move and create bonds with others. All these are essential for the development of curiosity, creativity and self-confidence and form the origins of Nurture. Throughout the remainder of childhood and into early adolescence, Nurture plays a very important role in our development as individuals. There are many scientific studies, opinions and arguments about what feeds into Nurture, but we can safely divide them into three main categories:

1. Parental

2. Social

3. Educational

1. Parental

A note here on terminology, I'm using the term 'parental', to represent primary caregivers, recognising that many people may not have been raised by their biological parents and, indeed, may have had different 'parental' influences throughout their upbringing.

Going back to our hunter-gatherer ancestors, remember the biggest factors in a child surviving into adulthood were parental protection, provision and influence. Our ancestors' role was to teach their children how to develop the skills required to look after themselves as they got older, which would ultimately determine the future success of the tribe.

Today we are no different. Studies reflect that parental influence plays a vital role in our readiness and preparedness for adult life.

I readily admit that parenting my three children is the thing I have found hardest in my life. I never know if I'm getting it quite right and, at times, think I've got it completely wrong. There is no manual (or reboot button).

Based on how impactful parental influence is on a child's nurture, it is very useful to know the areas our parenting has the greatest influence on:

- **Attachment Style – how we view and manage our relationships.**

- **Boundaries and Structure – how well we operate with rules and routines.**

- **Self-concept – how we view ourselves: our self-confidence and self-worth.**

- **Drive & Self-efficacy – how ambitious and conscientious we are.**

- **Locus of Control – the degree to which we believe we control our own lives.**

Given all this, it's fair to say that the way our parents parent us matters! In general, I do believe that in the majority of high-income economies we are 'sanitising' the experience of childhood to the extent that we are raising our children in a mental and physical ball of cotton wool, by no means readying them for the world they'll live in.

We are collectively making today's young people more comfortable and entitled, instead of more resilient and accountable. Given this, how can we expect them to understand consequences or self-awareness if we fail to provide, alongside safety and love, firm boundaries and an understanding of how to regulate their behaviour? If, through excess and comfort, our children have been able to avoid challenge and adversity, how can they learn to cope with the challenges of adulthood? How will they experience the rewards of delayed gratification or navigate feelings of disappointment if the answer to every request is 'Yes'? How will they learn to process discomfort, develop critical thinking, deal with their emotions, or understand and overcome fear, if all we do is remove it?

Parental influence is without question a critical element in the development of the knowledge, skills and abilities we so desperately need to deal with the challenge of being a modern-day human. Life isn't easy, it never has been. In fact, life is fucking hard and the more we prepare our children for this the better their prospects of a achieving a happy, productive and fulfilled life will be. How we behave in front of our children also has a profound effect.

Our children mirror and mimic us. By simply watching our behaviour the rooting of Drive, Self-efficacy and Locus of Control are established in their brains. Whereas Relationships, Boundaries and Self-concept are founded in personal experience and the parental approach to discipline and self-regulation.

All in all, you can now see how parental influence has a forceful impact on Nurture and the forming of a child's personality and world view.

2. Social

If parental influence is the main factor in forming personalities, this is closely followed by social exposure and experiences.

I'm talking about the wider environment, external of parental influence, outside the household or family group. It's the village, town or city where we grew up. The friends we chose, the hobbies and sports we pursued. Our friendship circles and their opinions. The interests and views of this collective, especially if the bonds were strong, can be incredibly influential in the choices we make throughout our teenage years and the repercussions this has on our personality type and world view.

Our Emotional Intelligence, or Emotional Quotient (EQ), is most tested, practised and developed in social situations. Our ability to navigate conflict, recognise and control our own emotions, pick up on other people's emotions and read group and power dynamics all evolve throughout our childhood and adolescent years, never more so than with friends and within relationships.

These are the years we build our database of reference points; what serves us well and what doesn't. Social influence plays a vital role in the development of our:

- **Emotional Intelligence – managing self, relationships and situations.**

- **Introversion vs Extroversion– learning what stimulates you and where you draw your energy from.**

- **Leadership vs Followship – how much control you need in group situations.**

- **Risk Threshold – your capacity for taking risks.**

- **Resilience – our ability to return to our baseline emotional state and bounce back after triumph or adversity.**

Friendship groups are incredibly important, as are cultural and societal expectations and norms. Fundamentally, this is our psychological playground away from parental oversight where we get to take risks, navigate relationships, make mistakes and find out where we fit in to group and power dynamics. What's also worth mentioning is that both parental and social influences significantly contribute to the political or religious beliefs we develop as adults.

In the UK, for example, if your parents hold left wing, socialist political views you are far more likely to hold those same beliefs as you enter adulthood. The same goes for the children whose parents believe in capitalism and hold more right wing political views. Of course, this is not the same for every individual, but electoral voting data from geographical demographics backs this up.

Just as parental influence impacts the forming of relationships, boundaries and locus of control, social exposure is incredibly influential in forming our approach to decision-making and risk, thus establishing our level of EQ. Parental and social influences combined also heavily affect the forming of our religious and political views and positions.

3. Educational

The third area of influence on our nurture is our experiences and influences from an educational perspective. This includes our academic experiences at school, college and university, together with external educational influences driven by access to wider resources, such as computers, smartphones and books, as well as education from parents and mentors.

Access to good education academically, technologically and socially is incredibly important and impacts our development and ability to better understand how the world around us works. Just as our social environment influences the forming of our EQ, our educational environment develops our Intelligence Quotient (IQ).

IQ tests assess things such as, verbal intelligence, mathematical ability, spatial awareness, visual and perception skills, working memory, logical reasoning, problem solving and pattern recognition. Yes, your baseline IQ can reflect your parent's biochemistry, meaning that you may well start off your educational years in a slightly gifted or disadvantaged position based on what's been passed down to you by mum and dad; however, it's the nurture element of education that will either support or stunt the potential for your IQ. Albert Einstein may well have started from a more elevated position genetically, but he needed education to take advantage of this. As did Steve Jobs, or any number of visionaries, business moguls and scientists.

Over the years a lot of research has been conducted around wealth, class and the impact of access to what's considered good education, because we know that educational influence plays a vital role in the development of:

- **Intelligence Quotient – the progression or regression of general intelligence.**

- **Learnability – the ability to absorb, process and apply new information to a current or future context.**

- **Discipline and Patience – the ability to remain focused and steadfast to achieve a result.**

- **Routine and Rigour – the ability to stick to a repetitive and not always enjoyable series of tasks.**

Just as parental and social influences play a large role in the forming of our adult personality type and view of the world, education is also a major contributing factor. Research suggests that IQ and Learnability are attributes largely gifted to us through our biochemistry, giving us a set starting point; however, our approach to Routine and Rigour, Discipline and Patience can be greatly influenced by the quantity and quality of our educational exposure.

Combining our Nature and Nurture

We have now established that our own personality types, characteristics and views of the world are established by the time we reach adulthood based on Nature, the genetics and biochemistry passed down from our parents, and Nurture, the influences and programming received through parental, social and educational influence. Given this we can see why we all respond differently to the three core functions of human existence. If we think for a moment about the seven billion people on the planet, their different cultures, languages and behavioural norms, we can also appreciate the massive variation of these differences, no less because Nature and Nurture do not work in isolation.

The interplay of Nature and Nurture

Working with a senior team at the Liverpool University Foundation Trust, I was speaking with a senior geneticist who explained to me the interplay between the two. Nature and Nurture interconnect throughout our early life, meaning that there are situations where your genetics can be influenced by your environment, just as, conversely, your perception of your environment can be influenced by your genetics. This was confirmed by studies at the Centre on the Developing Child at Harvard University that concluded the interactions between genes and environment do shape human development:

> "Despite the misconception that genes are set in stone, research shows that early experiences can determine how genes are turned on or off."[7]

For example, being around parents who smoke (environment) can alter the genes of the child. Family genetics have also been proven to factor in alcohol abuse (nature). In 2023, researchers at Indiana University School of Medicine discovered a group of genes that appear to influence pain and brain communication which in turn influence alcohol use[8], Further underlining the interplay between our genetics, gifted to us by our parents, and the environment we grow up in.

Let's now fast forward from early childhood to the age of 23–26 years old when, by and large, our adult brain is fully formed. We have navigated life to this point and through our nature and nurture have an established personality type. It's safe to say that we will continue to evolve, but the way we think, our mental foundations and approach to life, are established and deep seated.

This is a good moment to take some time to reflect on our own personality type. We've covered a lot in the initial few chapters, so with this emerging sense of our core functions of existence, the brain's motivation system, our three psychological states, plus our unique nature and nurture, what can we learn about ourselves? We can start by harnessing the power of the OCEAN.

Harnessing the power of the OCEAN

In psychology, the acronym OCEAN is widely used for assessing and identifying the 'big five' human personality traits. First developed by D. W. Fiske (1949), the OCEAN theory was later expanded upon by others including, Norman (1967), Smith (1967), Goldberg (1981) and McCrae and Costa (1987). OCEAN is also the model upon which many current psychometric profiling tests are based.

Posing a series of questions around five important personality traits, OCEAN represents:

 O = Openness: how open are you to the world, new experiences, new people and new ideas.

 C = Conscientiousness: your ability to stay goal focused, structured and avoid impulse or distraction.

 E = Extroversion: your level of extroversion vs introversion. Where you draw your energy from. People and social environments vs solace and personal space.

 A = Agreeableness: your natural levels of trust and good faith in others and your aversion to conflict vs your tendency to challenge, question and engage in conflict.

 N = Neuroticism: your susceptibility to anxiety and worry to potential threats in your daily life and how well you can deal with them.

There are many different psychometric profiling tools available today, from Myers-Briggs®, to Insight®, Strength Deployment Inventory® and PRINT® profiling but, one way or another, the majority incorporate questioning that is trying to draw out how you stack up against OCEAN.

For example, when tested, my OCEAN results were as follows:

O – I score high on my openness to try new things, new experiences and meet and interact with new people.

C – I score high on consciousness, meaning I can stay focused on a goal and have a good tolerance for avoiding impulse or distraction.

E – I score high for extroversion, meaning I draw my energy from being with people and in social situations, and enjoy expressing myself.

A – I score low on agreeableness, meaning that I'm more disagreeable; I want to question, challenge and debate things, especially if I have a difference of opinion or a strong position on something. Directly correlated with assertiveness, this low score has not always served me that well!

N – I score low on neuroticism, meaning that I am not overly susceptible to anxiety and worries in daily life and appear to have a high threshold for stress and duress. I suppose that may help with being rather disagreeable!

If we think back to the early chapters of this book, we explored survival, reproduction and purpose and how all our motivation stems from our evolutionary need to avoid pain and seek pleasure. In turn, this leads us to be in one of three psychological states at any one time: Neutral, Challenge or Threat. Which in turn causes us to take High or Low Road motivation activities. Well, now I can see exactly how this plays out for me in my adult life with my personality type.

My results tell me that I am hard-wired through evolution and programmed through my nature and nurture to embrace and perform well in Challenge and Threat State scenarios. In fact, I need High Road motivation activities in my life to feel motivated and fulfilled. After all, I love new experiences; I'm happy to work hard to get stuff done; I can stay goal focused, remain structured, on task and am not held back by anxiety. So, it sounds like I've cracked it right?

Well, no, not necessarily. My blind spots are also clear to see.

Firstly, I'm highly disagreeable by nature and nurture: I'm not always easy to be around especially if I am 'under the pump', under pressure, or worse, feeling overly attacked or challenged.

Secondly, I'm just not naturally wired for Neutral State. As we explored in earlier chapters the Neutral State plays a vital role in our ability to switch off, reset and recharge. It's also essential for the replenishment and uptake of dopamine. Yet, I struggle to find periods where I am in a true Neutral State. I often experience more anxiety when I'm at a loose end with no plans or no goal to drive towards. My wife has been the first to tell me over the years that I need to be more present and less distracted. She's right, of course, but then my disagreeable tendencies kick in, which means I become defensive without trying to address my behaviour.

You can see that my profiling shows I'm wired and motivated in ways which lend themselves well to navigating Challenge and Threat State situations relatively well. But, if I am going to balance the scales, which, ultimately, I must for my own well-being and those around me, I need to find time and space to feel comfortable and content being in a Neutral State. I must work out how I can be more content, relax and make time for things such as empathy and compassion. We will be looking at this later in the book.

You may be reading this now and thinking that you are the complete opposite. You are comfortable in Neutral State situations and are agreeable by nature, so from a humanistic and relationships perspective you have it all covered. Yet, you may also possess higher levels of neuroticism and lower levels of openness to new experiences and therefore you don't deal with Challenge or Threat States very well. That's fine, that's you! You are the combination of your natural genetics and your nurture experiences to date. But, to make the best of your potential, to be the best version of yourself, you need to find out how to balance your scales. You need to identify what changes you can make to perform better in the areas that don't serve you well, and the situations that can harm your well-being, relationships and personal fulfilment.

The work we do at T2 is so rewarding. We help people work out their adult motivations, characteristics and traits; we help them identify how they view situations and establish their view of the world. We help them uncover their trigger points, what they excel in, what they don't, and then strip it back to how they are likely to respond in survival mode (Threat State), identify what gives them purpose and fulfilment (Challenge State) and identify their capability to find comfort and contentment (Neutral State). With this knowledge people are able to feel more empowered to balance the scales in their lives, becoming more resilient and, as a result, are able to endure pain alongside experiencing true, meaningful pleasure.

Ok, let's find out what is really going on for you.

This is a great time for you to take the OCEAN test. Doing so is really going to help you as we move on through this book. If you don't choose to take the test, that's fine too, it's your choice and won't impact on the forthcoming chapters; however, personal test results can enrich your discovery and learning. You can loop back and take the test at any time.

Please follow the https://trans2performance.com/ocean to take your personal OCEAN profile test.

It will take around 10–15 minutes to complete. I recommend that you find a time and place to relax and focus on the test. Be honest. Your indicative results will show immediately at the end of the test. Please make sure you take a screen shot or note them down for later.

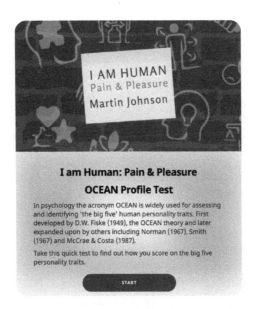

Free and secure, the OCEAN profiling is hosted by T2 website. Rest assured, your information will never be shared or sold by T2. Please visit our website for full privacy and security notice and contact details in case of difficulty.

Reflection

Read through your results carefully. Given what you discover, is it a surprise? What do you feel is supporting your life and what's potentially holding you back? Is it clear cut?

All the same, but very different!

"We are all different. There is no such thing as a standard or run-of-the-mill human being, but we share the same human spirit."

Stephen Hawking[9]

The reasons you are you stem from a unique combination of your nature and nurture. Yet, despite this complexity of genes and environmental programming, when you strip us all back, we are still all governed by the same three core functions of human existence. We have a need to survive and avoid threat. We have a need to reproduce and raise our offspring. We need to have a purpose and a role in life. The complexity of our personality types and characteristics, however, fundamentally affect how we react and respond to these three core functions. This explains why some of us excel under pressure and some don't. Why some naturally take to parenting and others don't. Why some of us have natural drive and ambition and others don't.

So how does your nature and nurture impact the way you interact with the wider world? What is the net result of all your genetic and environmental programming?

We're now going to take a dive into your world view to better understand what this is and how it plays a pivotal role in your ability to endure pain and enjoy pleasure. Lets head there right away…

Chapter 4

Your World View

How it was formed and where you fit in.

What do I mean by world view?

Your world view has two distinct parts: the first is your current mental model of how the world is organised, structured and works. It's your unique perceived framework for how the world operates. The second is how much, or how little, you buy into or agree with that framework. Your world view matters because it feeds into your ability to endure pain and uncertainty in Threat State, seek the pleasure and reward of the Challenge State or just rest and recuperate in Neutral State.

Different for each of us, for the most part our world view is created by our responses to five key questions:

1. **How do I believe the world was created?** Our religious or scientific position.

2. **How do I believe the world operates?** Our political, societal, environmental position.

3. **Do I agree with or accept how the world operates?** Our acceptance position.

4. **What are my motivations and values?** Our moral position.

5. **What happens to us when we die?** Our spiritual or
   evolutionary position.

Over thousands of years of human evolution, the world has become a diverse, multicultural place. We have seen the emergence of faith-based religions and scientific understanding, along with the establishment of cultural, political, and societal norms. What follows are ten examples of the type of thinking that contributes to the formation of a world view.

Humanism: the world is a natural place based on science and reason.

Pantheism: the world was created by God or a supreme entity.

Optimism: the world is my oyster; hope is key, and anything is possible.

Pessimism: the world is corrupt; I trust very few people.

Moralism: the world should be fair and just; we should share the same morals and values.

Moral Subjectivism: the world is morally indifferent; morals and values are all subjective.

Individualism: I will control my own destiny; I will be self-reliant and make my own success.

Collectivism: things should be done together and for the greater good of all.

Stoicism: I must be strong and endure the pain and challenge of life.

Entitleism: I deserve to have what I want. I deserve pleasure, reward and happiness.

World view and its influence on pain and pleasure

I'm now going to look at two people and their different world views. From their answers to the big five questions, I'm going to unpick how this plays out in their lives. Anonymised to protect their identities, these are two subjects from our T2 studies.

Sarah answered the five questions as follows:

1. **How do I believe the world was created?**

   "*I believe in science, evolution and the Big Bang theory.*"

2. **How do I believe the world operates?**

   "*I believe that the world operates largely through global capitalism and economies and is largely controlled by those who are in positions of power. My political persuasion is centre right, and I believe that all people on Earth could thrive and be successful. Despite this I do believe that there are those who are not as fortunate as others or who are vulnerable and disadvantaged and therefore should be looked after.*"

3. **Do I agree with or accept how the world operates?**

   "*Yes, I think on balance this has been proven for thousands of years as the most sustainable way to evolve and progress as a species. Although there are still lots of areas human beings can improve on and progress in, we are yet to find a better alternative.*"

4. **What are my motivations and values?**

   "*I am motivated by freedom, to be in control of my destiny and be self-reliant. I'm also motivated to succeed, achieve and take advantage of the capitalist world we live in whilst securing financial security and contributing to that world in a positive way.*"

5. **What happens to us when we die?**
    *"I believe that we are a living organism that ultimately ages
    and dies. The prospect of any life after death is therefore
    unlikely in my opinion. Although I hope I'm wrong I'm
    comfortable with mortality and death."*

Sarah's world view appears to consist of the following elements:
Humanism | Optimism | Individualism | Stoicism

**Let's look now at the pros and cons of Sarah's world view and how
it would play out in terms of her relationship with pain and pleasure.**

Pros: given that Sarah's world view is somewhat aligned with the
reality of the way the world currently operates (whether that is
a good or a bad thing is a different question), she is less likely to
become angry, resentful and distracted by the challenges of day-
to-day life. She also believes that her happiness and success is in
her own hands. Sarah understands that the world is imperfect and
there is suffering, she also has an acceptance of human mortality.
This will naturally make for a more resilient mindset.

Cons: Sarah's world view is built for self-reliance, control and
endurance. Although this is a good thing in terms of dealing with
challenges, it does not lend itself to catering for the needs of others,
self-sacrifice, the greater good or collaboration. This is not to say
that Sarah can't do these things, but they are not important to her.
Her world view also doesn't lend itself to sometimes stopping and
enjoying the simple things in life, such as nature, relationships and
simple impactful moments.

Sarah's relationship with pain and pleasure has the potential to be
balanced and work well for her, however, with her current world view she
would have to be careful that she doesn't fall into a pattern of behaviour
that constitutes constant pain endurance and a Challenge State. Yes, she
is built to be resilient but if continuous, even Sarah's capacity to cope well
will be overwhelmed and exhausted. She must make time to enjoy and
appreciate her life and rest and recharge in her Neutral State. Sarah also

needs to understand that, although this is her world view, there are many other views that are built on different principles and beliefs that are just as valid and useful.

Now let's look at John. He answered the five questions as follows:

1. **How do I believe the world was created?**
   "I believe in religion and the existence and guiding principles of a higher power."

2. **How do I believe the world operates?**
   "I believe that the world operates largely through global capitalism and economies controlled by those who are in positions of power. My political persuasion is on the left, and I believe in socialism and democracy. I am also a pacifist. I think the world operates very differently to my ideals and only benefits the rich and powerful. I believe there is systemic injustice and inequality in the world."

3. **Do I agree with or accept how the world operates?**
   "In the main, no, I don't. Although I still take time to appreciate the good in life and try to remain focused on my family, friends and the things that matter to me, I feel the world is in a worse place now than it was a few years ago and becoming worse for future generations. I remain guarded and sceptical about those in power."

4. **What are my motivations and values?**
   "I am motivated to be a good human, believe in and follow my faith and to try and make a difference in the world."

5. **What happens to us when we die?**
   "I believe in God and my religion and I believe that there is life after death, whether that be in spirit or through reincarnation."

John's world view appears to consist of the following elements:
Pantheism | Moralism | Collectivism | Pessimism

Again, let's look now at the pros and cons of John's world view and how it would play out in terms of his relationship with pain and pleasure.

Pros: John's world view is very different to Sarah's. John sees the world through his faith and, ultimately, as a place where humans should work together for the common good, displaying similar morals and values. With this world view John is likely to be highly altruistic and put the needs of others before himself, offering service to those less fortunate. He has a strong belief in right and wrong, is anti-conflict with high levels of empathy for human suffering and inequality. John believes in life after death, if he lives by the morals and principles of his faith. This world view naturally lends itself to humanistic and idealistic philosophy. John is probably most comfortable amongst people he trusts and with those who share similar views.

Cons: whilst John's world view has plenty of positives, it can also present him with difficulties. John's is not as aligned with the world's political and systemic way of operating. This is likely to present many challenges and frustrations for John. He doesn't believe in the systems of capitalism and power to be just, neither does he agree with war to solve international conflict. John's faith is strong and aspects of life like injustice and crime are troubling. As a result, John has the potential to become mistrustful, guarded and paranoid of people and situations. This results in hypersensitivity to perceived threats, never mind real threats, and this could inhibit John's ability to take risks and achieve goals.

John's relationship with pain and pleasure has the potential to be balanced and work well for him, however, given his world view John is highly susceptible to mistrust and scepticism. This can lead to periods of frustration and resentment, putting himself in a regular and recurring Threat State. This in turn may reduce his ability to push into Challenge State situations and lead to him to seek the Neutral State more often. John will, however, enjoy deep human connections with those close to him and who share his beliefs. John will appreciate moments and experiences and always try to do the right thing by himself and others. Just like Sarah, however, John needs to remember and think about the many other world views that are built on different principles and beliefs that are just as valid and useful.

Balancing our world views

From these two examples you can start to appreciate how our world view feeds directly into our ability to endure pain and uncertainty in Threat State, seek the pleasure and reward of the Challenge State and offer important rest and recuperate in Neutral State. All three of these are required for us humans to fulfil our three core functions of existence: survival, reproduction and purpose.

There are many different variations and unique combinations of world view; some more aligned with the way the current world operates and some not at all; some more aligned with Challenge and Threat situations and others aligned to remaining in Neutral State situations. However, the important thing to realise is that:

Our world view is born out of our nature and nurture.

The combination of genetics and environment that we explored in the last chapter, our nature and nurture, is instrumental in the formulation of our world view.

At T2 we conduct many interviews and 1-2-1 sessions capturing thousands of data points. When people talk about the challenges and frustrations in their life, or when they explain why they believe they're struggling mentally, almost without exception, their world view is the root cause. Something is out of line with the way they see the world and, as a result, their ability to balance pain and pleasure in their lives becomes compromised.

Sometimes they are in a period of perpetual Threat State, making routine, daily experiences difficult and exhausting. Sometimes they are feeling overwhelmed or burnt out, because of putting themselves in a relentless Challenge State with workload. Sometimes they have got themselves in a situation where they have programmed themselves to be in a perpetual Neutral State, craving security and contentment. This, however, then leads to them becoming unfulfilled, as they can no longer push themselves into any remotely challenging situations, resulting in the dopamine depletion and comfort crisis we explored earlier in the book.

Understanding your world view really matters because it forms your current mental model of how the world is organised, structured and works. In turn, it governs how much, for better or worse, you buy into and agree with that framework.

The biggest contributing factors that form your world view are your nature and nurture – the complex combination of the genetics passed down to you from your parents and the environment you grew up in during your early years of brain development. All of which are underpinned by the need to fulfil those three core functions of human existence: survival, reproduction and purpose.

Time to get better acquainted with your world view

Following on from the OCEAN test in the last chapter, it's now time to get more clarity around your world view. So, before we venture any further, it's going to be well worth your time putting this book down and spending some time learning more about yourself.

Please visit www.trans2performance.com/worldview and complete the short questionnaire.

This free tool will give you an indication of your current world view. You will receive your results on completion of the test. **Please screen shot or make a note of them.**

Although you don't need to take this test to continue with the book, having an indication of your world view at this point will enrich your self-discovery and we will return to these results later in the book.

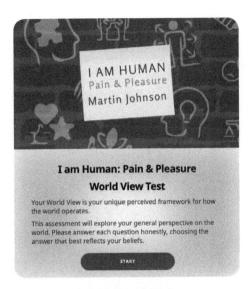

Free and secure, World View profiling is hosted by T2 website. Rest assured, your information will never be shared or sold by T2. Please visit our website for full privacy and security notice and contact details in case of difficulty.

Next, we're going to circle back to pain and pleasure. We need to better understand just what it takes to endure or experience them, how to make best use of both and what they teach us about our lives.

Chapter 5

Enduring Pain

How personal characteristics and attributes can make all the difference.

It's not just our ability to experience pleasure that defines us, but more our ability to endure suffering that really counts. Earlier we described 'pain' as both a mental and physical sensation: it feels uncomfortable, challenging or painful and leads us to move away from or avoid whatever gives us these sensations.

We're now going to look into pain and pleasure and identify the personal characteristics and attributes required to both endure and seek them.

An attribute is defined as a quality, characteristic or inherent trait that a person possesses. At T2 we've spent many years identifying, testing and developing human beings' attributes and motivators. In 2023, we partnered with The Attributes Inc., a US-based consultancy founded and led by former Navy SEAL Commander Rich Diviney. A veteran of 20 years' military service, Diviney was involved in the specialised SEAL selection process. Through this work he cracked the code of human performance in an elite military environment and wrote the best-seller *The Attributes: 25 Hidden Drivers of Optimal Performance*.

Diviney discovered that, beyond the obvious physical and practical skills a SEAL recruit demonstrated, ultimately, it was their psychological attributes that were most important in successful selection. Diviney then embarked on a process of identifying the common attributes shared by successful candidates to create a blueprint for assessment and development. Drawing on our T2 research and utilising some of the definitions and understanding from Diviney's work, we're now going to explore the key characteristics and attributes required to endure pain and discomfort.

Before we dive in, it's worth mentioning that attributes and traits are innate and, as we explored in the last chapter, are dependent on our nature and nurture. This means we enter adulthood with a baseline level for each one. According to Diviney, an attribute may register as low, moderate or high. It doesn't mean, however, that we cannot improve an attribute; it also doesn't mean that we cannot regress with a particular attribute either. Through our unique nature and nurture, however, we'll be starting at a particular baseline position with each one.

Ok, let's get started. When it comes to enduring pain and either pushing into Challenge State or dealing with Threat State, we need four key attributes: Courage, Durability, Resilience and Persistence.

Courage
The catalyst for pushing into pain and discomfort.

Courage is not the absence fear, it's the ability to face difficulty, uncertainty or danger despite it.

In fact, if there was no fear, we'd have no need for courage. Given that survival is our number one core function, with our fight or flight response designed to help us stay alive, fear is a very natural and important psychological response. We are, therefore, hard-wired for courage. As a species, we wouldn't have survived very long without it. However, as we have explored, depending on our nature, nurture and world view, some of us will naturally possess higher levels of courage than others; some will have moderate levels and some of us may be low on courage. This explains why some people can push into Challenge and Threat State situations more easily than others. It's also why some are more comfortable engaging in High Road motivation scenarios, drawing on their natural ability to push into discomfort and endure pain.

We all have some level of courage, and the great news is that if you are low or moderate on courage, you can improve.

Today, I absolutely love speaking to large audiences. I get such a buzz from it, but this wasn't always the case. Far from it! When I first started speaking at events, I was absolutely terrified. I knew I wanted to do it and I accepted that I would feel uncomfortable; I also knew that it would take everything I had to get up on a stage and speak, and not just the first time but many times after that. If I am being honest, it took years for me to become remotely comfortable, but I wanted and needed to conquer my fear. It's only now some 800+ speaking gigs later that I truly enjoy the experience of public speaking and look forward to the challenge and feedback from each and every one.

I overcame my fear and built courage through a psychological process called 'desensitisation'. Essentially you can desensitise yourself to the effects of a fearful situation by reprogramming your brain to think: it's fine, it's perfectly safe or – even better – it's productive and enjoyable, and here's how.

Three steps to desensitisation

1. Exposure
When we first experience an uncertain, challenging or dangerous situation.

2. Repetition
The action of repeating our exposure.

3. Programming
Our brain's creation of neural pathways, or memories, about the situation.

The first step is the hardest! It takes all your courage, whatever level of courage that represents, but this first exposure is so important. Whether, like me, it was speaking in public for the first time or maybe, for you, it might involve confronting a friend about their behaviour; getting on a plane; picking up a spider; or being confined to a small space... Whatever creates fear in your mind, the first exposure is crucial because you need to push into your fear and face the situation in order to get started. If, in that first moment, you bail out and avoid the situation, this only serves to exacerbate your fear next time around, so facing it is key. Next comes step two and the power of repetition for building higher levels of courage.

Repeated exposure will gradually reduce the fear response, as you start to realise that "it ain't so bad!" Step two, naturally overlaps with step three because, with every repeated exposure, you are creating new neural pathways in your brain that give you greater understanding, more knowledge and a less severe reaction to something that once scared the life out of you.

When I entered the military, our training was packed with exercises and tasks designed to desensitise us to the type of activities we would have to encounter should we serve in the real world. We were exposed to difficult situations that would naturally trigger a Threat State in us. Whether that was jumping from a helicopter; firing live weapons; crawling through a tight space (my personal nemesis); being submerged in water with heavy clothing or abseiling from a significant height. It was exposure to, and repetition of, these situations that enabled us to desensitise ourselves to their effects.

Although you may not be jumping out of a helicopter or navigating a half-submerged tunnel in the dark, you may be plucking up the courage to deal with conflict, conquer your fear of heights, or: deliver better presentations at work, all of which may trigger a fight or flight response in your mind and body. We are anxious because it could go wrong; we don't want to deal with the conflict or consequences; our hearts are pounding, our palms sweaty... For those who just don't like uncertainty or danger, or who have a fear of rejection or judgement, it all equates to the same thing. Courage is required.

"He who is brave is free."

Seneca[10]

Courage is the catalyst for pushing into pain and discomfort.

Now, if you are reading this and think that you may be low or moderate on Courage, then consider when and where you can put yourself into situations that may develop it. Start small. Follow the three-step process and achieve desensitisation and, if you practise, you can set your brain on a path to a greater tolerance of pain and discomfort.

Durability

The ability to endure pain and discomfort.

Durability is the ability to endure pain and discomfort for a sustained period beyond our brains' natural pain threshold. Our pain thresholds are based on sensitivity to sound and temperature, gender, age and genetics, meaning that, again, we are all different when it comes to our natural level of durability in an uncomfortable or painful situation. Differing from person to person, I find that durability is generally low/moderate for most people I work with. After all, the ability to avoid pain has played a huge role in our survival and evolution.

It's worth noting that there are two types of durability: physical and psychological. Studies show that although physical and psychological pain can fluctuate and differ, they are often connected. For example, a person may be robust and display a high level of durability with physical pain but could struggle with psychological pain, and vice versa. However, by and large, our level of durability to pain and discomfort is consistently connected, both physically and psychologically.

We can control our pain by how we respond to it.

Our minds can either moderate or intensify pain, meaning how we process what's happening around us and to us, and what we do with that information really matters. Those of us who can mentally compartmentalise challenges and push forward are often able to lessen pain and discomfort through the following three steps:

1. **Acknowledgement**
   Fully accept the situation is uncomfortable.

2. **Relaxation**
   Consciously relax the body.

3. **Distraction**
   Take the mind to a different place.

Most humans instinctively want to push pain and discomfort away. We've all been there, awake at night worrying about stuff and, more often than not, trying to ignore or block out these worrying thoughts, but they seem to continue coming back and the sleepless hours tick by as we spiral down mental wormholes. What we must do instead is acknowledge these worries and establish why they are there in the first place. Taking a minute to process and acknowledge them really helps.

A good example would be if you decided to run a marathon and you admit to yourself right from the start that it's going to hurt and hurt a lot. If you do this, you'll have a much greater chance of completing the distance because, when the pain really starts to kick in and negative thoughts arise, you are more prepared having already acknowledged and accepted that this is part and parcel of the job in hand. On the contrary, if you think it's going to be a breeze and don't prepare accordingly, you're likely to hit a huge brick wall mentally and physically, because the surprise of the unwanted and unexpected pain and discomfort overwhelms you.

The second technique for building durability in pain and discomfort is relaxation. We must physically relax the body. With a fight or flight response our bodies are primed and readied for action: adrenaline and cortisol flood the brain, blood flows to our muscles, our vision tunnels and our breathing speeds up, all in a bid to ready us for battle. This brings with it tension and with tension comes more adrenaline and cortisol and, therefore, the cycle can repeat. In stressful and painful situations, consciously relaxing the body can help with durability. A great way of achieving this is to drop your shoulders, which are likely to be around your ears at this point, let your tongue fall to the base of your mouth and then just focus on slowing your breathing down. As you drop your shoulders, allow your tongue to fall and relax your jaw, your whole body will begin to relax.

Finally, to supercharge your levels of durability, you must master the art of distracting your mind. This is one of the most important and best techniques for the endurance of pain and discomfort. After acknowledging the issue and relaxing the body, consciously taking your mind away from the pain and discomfort by thinking about something else will allow you to sustain pain and discomfort. And for much longer than your brain would naturally allow.

"Some of us think holding on makes us strong; but sometimes it is letting go."

Hermann Hesse[11]

Whether you are on a long training run for a marathon; exposed to cold water therapy; having a tough time with a colleague at work, or just struggling with where your life is heading, the ability to acknowledge the situation for what it is without pushing it away, consciously taking a moment to relax and then distract the mind by taking it somewhere else, significantly enhances your ability to be durable. Easier said than done, of course, and I'm sure you'll have any number of situations in mind from your life. But, if you are going to endure pain and discomfort, you must make a conscious decision to intervene in your body's natural response through acknowledgement, relaxation and distraction.

Resilience

The ability to bounce back following pain and discomfort.

Resilience is the ability to rapidly return to our baseline emotional and mental state after a stressful, traumatic or even triumphant event.

Think of an elastic band. It has a shape and when stretched the band becomes longer and more taut. If you then release the tension, the band returns to its original form because it has a high level of resilience.

In contrast, if you hold a ball of modelling clay in your hand and squeeze it hard, once you let go it will not return to its original form because the substance it's made of has a low level of resilience. It can't perform in the same way as the elastic band.

In Challenge or Threat States we are psychologically pushing ourselves outside our comfort zone, and in turn, this triggers our fight or flight response, leaving us feeling wary, anxious or compromised. Those who have a high level of resilience will tend to deal with these situations by following the steps we explored around courage and durability and, as a result, they very quickly return to their baseline emotional and mental state – or as we explored earlier, their Neutral State. The same applies if they achieve something fulfilling and elating; they take time to appreciate and celebrate it and then return to baseline and their Neutral State very quickly.

Those who are low on resilience, however, don't possess the same ability to return to their baseline quickly. After encountering a Threat or Challenge State situation, their fight or flight triggers an elevated emotional state, yet it takes them some time to return to their baseline. This can vary from person to person. For some it may take hours to recover, for some it may be days! Either way, their mind and body systems get stuck in an overly heightened state of alertness, anxiety or euphoria – a suboptimal situation for them, especially if they need to focus on a new task or push into the same situation or activity again any time soon.

Like other characteristics and attributes, we all have a starting position when it comes to our levels of resilience. These levels are naturally preset by our genetics and embedded through our parental influence and our environment – our nurture. However, we can develop greater levels of resilience through exposure to different situations followed by some quick techniques applied in the aftermath. Two useful techniques include:

1. **Start the Clock**

2. **ABC Technique**

First, let's look at the Start the Clock technique. When we are exposed to a Challenge or Threat State situation and our fight or flight kicks in, we need to take back control of our minds. When I interviewed Rich Diviney at the 2023 T2 Leadership Retreat, I asked him, *"Is there anything practical you applied in your military career to improve your resilience?"*

He answered, *"Well, we used to have a simple technique called the Two Minute Rule. If we experienced adversity or challenge, we would give ourselves two minutes to moan, rant and cuss. We would get it all off our chest. Then, after two minutes we would forget about it and move forward with the job in hand."* He then went on to say, *"The same rule applied for when we experienced triumph or victory. We would give ourselves two minutes to whoop, high five and celebrate and then after two minutes we would get back to our job."*

This approach allowed the Navy SEALs to acknowledge their emotions, but importantly, it meant they could regain control quickly; essentially conditioning their minds to become more resilient in the face of both adversity and triumph. They were forming a habit of returning to their baseline state efficiently time after time, no matter what was happening.

Here at T2 we also teach a return-to-baseline technique to elite sports men and women who regularly compete under extreme pressure. We also teach it to emergency service responders, frontline workers and even business executives. The technique is called ABC and stands for: Acknowledge – Breathe – Control.

Just as with Durability, acknowledging the situation is crucial.

With **durability,** you are acknowledging what is happening in the moment in order to **endure** it.

With **resilience**, you are acknowledging what has just happened in order to **process** it.

If you don't acknowledge and accept it, your mind will be focused on excitement, resentment or panic, and you will ultimately struggle to get back to your baseline state.

Once you have acknowledged a situation, slow your breathing down for 90 seconds.

In her book *My Stroke of Insight*, leading neuroscientist Jill Bolte Taylor[12] discovered that the effects of chemicals like cortisol released into the brain to create the fight or flight response, last for around 90 seconds. So, if we pause and focus on our breath for 90 seconds and literally do nothing, our brain's chemical spike will fade. This also goes a long way to explaining why Diviney's Two Minute Rule also works so well.

Just taking time to slow down your breathing for 90 seconds will allow you to **clear the mind to take control** and reduce the potential of feeling victimised, overly euphoric or anxious that only serves to set off another release of brain chemicals which will again heighten the system .

Once back at your baseline you can focus on the things you control and what actions you need to take, to either help you move past or deal with the situation. I also just want to say that, depending on your situation and preset attributes, give yourself space and time – you may need ten minutes, not 90 seconds. The results, however, are the same.

"Do not judge me by my success, judge me by how many times I fell down and got back up again."

Nelson Mandela[13]

ABC: (Acknowledge – Breathe – Control) is a simple yet highly effective technique to help us move forwards and return to our baseline state, and with it, develop a much greater level of resilience through conscious habit.

Persistence

The desire to try again and again despite delay in reducing the pain and discomfort.

To be persistent is to keep doing something, even though it doesn't feel like it's getting any easier or more comfortable.

Each of us require a different amount of exposure to achieve an adequate level of desensitisation and some of us will require higher levels of persistence than others. For example: you have recently been promoted to a managerial position in your workplace and have been avoiding addressing the under performance of certain team members for a while. The thought of conflict is making you feel uneasy to the point of sickness. You're not sleeping and are experiencing real anxiety around it.

You finally pluck up the **courage** to have the first conversation with a team member and it goes as poorly as you suspected it would. You are met with challenge and conflict, and nothing is resolved. However, you have achieved the first exposure and saw the meeting through with some **durability**. You now need to demonstrate some **resilience** to bounce back from that first exposure and its lack of impact, steady yourself, return to baseline and be committed to follow through on your next actions.

You then demonstrate both courage and durability again as you arrange to speak with the second person in the team and repeat the cycle. And guess what? It's not feeling any easier at this point either. The performance reviews with these individuals are now happening monthly but the improved results you're looking for are not materialising, meaning that each interaction remains difficult and uncomfortable. You are going to have to demonstrate an abundance of persistence to repeat and continue the process until you eventually reach your desired outcome.

"Paralyze resistance with persistence."

Woody Hayes[14]

For one person these interactions may get easier after the first three or four times, as they quickly start to become desensitised to their effects. For another it may take 10 or 12 interactions and even then, they still may feel as nervous as they did at the start. However, in both cases it's persistence they'll need. Sooner or later both people will desensitise but at different rates and stages. Both, however, still require high levels of persistence to stay committed to enduring the pain and discomfort time and again.

What's holding you back?

If you are high on persistence, naturally you are more likely to be able to push into Challenge State situations and deal with Threat State situations quite well. If you are low or moderate on persistence, then you need to try and identify why that may be the case.

What is your nemesis when it comes to persistence?

Let's look at three of the biggest inhibitors to persistence:

Fear of Failure

We know from our testing here at T2, specifically through a tool called PRINT® profiling, that all humans have unconscious and differing motivators. Some of these motivators can result in a fear of failure. In fact, their fear of looking bad, being embarrassed or losing is so great that it can lead to them avoiding situations where the chances of this happening are high. Think about the example of our new manager: if they cannot deal with difficult characters in the team effectively, then they will start to lose their credibility or maybe worse, their job. So, the easier road may be to just avoid the situation altogether, in the hope that it can somehow be contained, or that it will sort itself out eventually.

Impatience

Some of us are impatient (me, more than most), which basically means that we have an intolerance or irritability with anything that impedes or delays us from reaching a desired outcome. Again, for our new manager the results they want are not appearing, along with the feeling that there is no progress with these team members, at least not early on. If they are low on patience, and are therefore impatient, they will tend to want to be more bullish about resolving the situation and could end up making it worse. Impatience could also result in them withdrawing from the situation entirely, as they just don't want to waste their time or energy on something they see as unproductive. This approach, however, is counterproductive and, again, doesn't resolve the issue at hand.

High Neuroticism

Earlier in the book we looked at OCEAN profiling and hopefully you took time to take the online test. The N in OCEAN stands for Neuroticism, which represents your natural susceptibility to stress, worry and anxiety. If you are low on neuroticism you should possess the ability to push into pain and discomfort with high levels of persistence, because the effects of the pain and discomfort are not likely to be as uncomfortable. If you are high on neuroticism, then the degree to which pain and discomfort will affect you will naturally be greater. In some, this could be so overwhelming, or indeed crippling, in that it completely inhibits the level of persistence required to continue dealing with the pain and discomfort. This can naturally result, not only in a withdrawal of engagement, but also in that person's stress and anxiety levels rising to a point where it can affect their mental well-being.

Although, as we've established, we're all different through our nature, nurture and world view, it is a universal requirement that all of us must be able to condition ourselves to endure pain and discomfort throughout our lives. We must be able to resolve conflict, conquer our personal fears, push ourselves into challenging situations, manage our negative thoughts and make difficult decisions. In order to do these things, we need to be able to develop the attributes and characteristics required to endure pain and discomfort:

Courage – Durability – Resilience – Persistence

If we are going to achieve this we must first establish if we are naturally low, moderate or high on these attributes.

The results from your OCEAN test and World View assessment will give you an indication, and it's highly likely that you have a gut feeling on where you stack up.

I invite you to put this book down and take another optional quick test, visit www.theattributes.com and take Rich Diviney's 42 Attributes Assessment™.

Amongst others, you will be able to get feedback on whether you score as low, moderate or high for Courage, Durability, Resilience and Persistence. When you've completed the test, take a moment to consider:

Do your results match with how you feel about yourself?

Were you surprised?

What's resonating and why?

Knowledge is power!

We have now explored the characteristics and attributes required to endure pain and discomfort, so let's push on and explore those required to seek out and receive pleasure and reward. It's now time to start getting motivated by the art of the possible.

Chapter 6

Seeking Pleasure

The greatest rewards are often on the other side of difficulty.

Before we begin, let's first recap what we mean by pleasure. Both a mental and physical sensation, a feeling of comfort, contentment and reward, pleasure leads us to seek and repeat whatever action gives us this sensation in the first place.

When we choose High Road motivation, which offers delayed relief, results, gains or gratification, and perform in our Challenge State, once the desired outcome is achieved, we experience a sense of pleasure and reward greater than the comfort and contentment we experience in our Neutral State. Those who form a habit of this behaviour tend to have higher levels of certain attributes, our innate traits which are driven by our nature and nurture.

Drive

The need or desire to achieve an outcome.

I find it interesting that many people think that it's the attribute of Vision (which we will come to next) that comes before Drive when we form a plan to try to achieve something, when really, it's the other way around. Drive is the catalyst for pushing us into situations that will deliver pleasure and reward.

Remember earlier in the book when I discussed the brain chemical dopamine? We established that dopamine is the motivation molecule behind all our decisions and actions, not the result of them. When our need for something is strong, dopamine floods the brain, creating the motivation and energy to act upon our desire. Drive is, therefore, our inner desire or need to achieve something meaningful or necessary.

Drive is a crucial attribute for experiencing pleasure and reward. After all, without it we would not muster the motivation to do anything.

Some of us are naturally high on drive, some have moderate levels and some low. Think back to our hunter-gatherer ancestors for a minute, their drive was born largely out of a necessity to survive and provide. They needed to provide food, safety and shelter, which ultimately mobilised them into action. You could argue that in our modern-day, high-income economies we still have the same primal drivers. While this may be true, the urgency behind daily provision and responsibility is not as great for us as it was for our ancestors. For example, we have a social and benefits system, a healthcare system, parental and charitable support, and so on. For us, drive is necessary, but from a core function perspective, not the necessity it once was. The life or death repercussions of inaction are not as prevalent.

When we consider our evolutionary and biological make-up, it's our drive to achieve something meaningful or necessary that leads to significant pleasure and reward. For us modern-day humans, drive expands beyond our basic needs; it's not just about survival and provision, it's the force behind achieving our personal goals, careers, aspirations and relationships.

Those who are low to moderate on drive cannot simply manufacture it out of thin air, but what they can do is ask themselves some questions around their own internal sense of purpose. This may help them connect with something that results in an increased level of drive and with it the motivation to act.

Throughout my coaching sessions and interactions across all high-performance environments, the people I meet and work with almost always have a high degree of drive fuelled by a clear and distinct sense of purpose.

To help us understand our purpose and establish what that may be right now, the following four categories are the most common examples we come across at T2. I explore them in detail in my first book *I am Human: 30 Mistakes to Success*[15] , they are:

- **To avoid** failure embarrassment or struggle. Driven by fear this is the most powerful sense of purpose. It may stem from early life experiences: going without, adversity or being exposed to toxic or harsh environments.

- **To prove** someone right or wrong. Driven by fear and desire, again this strong sense of purpose comes from having a point to prove based on our treatment by others: parents, siblings, teachers. It may be a sense of injustice, or alternatively, proving someone right because of their belief in us.

- **To achieve** something significant and tangible. Driven by desire, centred on gaining something tangible for our efforts, this sense of purpose takes the form of legacy: a qualification, an award, a promotion or our name on the door.

- **To provide** for those who depend on me. Driven by both fear and desire, this sense of purpose is centred around the need to provide for ourselves and those that matter to us, whether that's comfort, security, material possessions or education. The need to replicate or exceed a standard of living and/or care we either did, or did not, experience ourselves.

If you connect with any of the above four statements, then it's likely that you have a moderate to high drive.

The origins of my drive lie firmly in wanting to avoid failure, embarrassment and struggle, whilst also trying to prove a few select people wrong! And because to avoid and prove is so strong in me, I'm propelled towards High Road motivation and continually push into Challenge State. It's here that I find true pleasure when I achieve my endeavours and am rewarded with results.

If Drive creates the need or desire to propel us towards an outcome, it's Vision that pushes us on to the next stage. After all, when the idea is hot and our emotion high, we tend to act!

Vision

The foresight and imagination of achieving an outcome.

If Drive is the catalyst for achieving an outcome, Vision brings the outcome alive in the mind.

Our ability to imagine an outcome is what separates us from any other species on Earth. How we can build a mental image of the future and pre-live how that moment may look and feel is such an important attribute for seeking and experiencing pleasure and reward. This is because the moment we start to visualise a rewarding outcome in our minds, our brains release dopamine, and bingo! We're already experiencing a hit of pleasure at the sheer thought of receiving pleasure; we physically respond to the excitement and anticipation of what a rewarding outcome might look and feel like.

"If you can see it, you can be it."

Billy Jean King[16]

I have worked with many elite athletes and teams, the most successful of which are incredibly high on the attribute of Vision. They envisage training milestones, defining moments, receiving medals or lifting the trophies. Their use of imagery is second-to-none. What I have also discovered is that they are not just tapping into their imaginations to feel the satisfaction of hitting training goals or the achievement of victory. Many high-performing individuals also use it to envisage how they would overcome challenge and adversity. Either way, it is this visualisation or mental practice, that enables them to start preparing their brain for what's to come and significantly contributes to and increases their chances of resilience and success.

Studies have shown that a combination of mental and physical practice greatly enhances a person's ability to perform and master a skill. Brain scans reveal that the same area of the brain is activated when we think about a task, as when we undertake it. One such study looked at a group of novice golfers and found that a combination of mental and physical practice helped them perform better than those who only undertook physical practice[17]. This technique is also useful for helping to reduce anxiety and increase confidence, from musicians and weightlifters to surgeons, this phenomenon is useful for enhancing different skill sets, including people recovering movement in their limbs after a stroke[18].

To use this technique it's important to give yourself as clear a goal as you can and as much mental stimulus as possible, for example:

- Have a specific goal or outcome in mind. This may be a skill you are trying to master, a difficult meeting you are planning, a shot on goal or a public speaking engagement. Write it down, collect data, do your research and map it out then…

- Find a quiet, comfortable place that you won't be disturbed.

- Give yourself time to slow your breathing and focus.

- Mentally go through the task ahead of you and as you do this…

- Engage each of your five senses: sight, smell, sound, touch and taste. Use each one to visualise your surroundings and bodily sensations. Where are you? What does it smell like? What does your body feel like? Are you calm and confident? What are you wearing?

- Repeat and adapt your visualisation regularly to support your goal.

Making the vision as rich and real as possible will help it be more effective. In reality, of course, the outcome may not match our vision, but by visualising positive outcomes in advance, we can give ourselves the best chance of preparing ourselves mentally and physically for success.

Some of the most successful and influential people in history were great visionaries. Possessing the ability to visualise a different or innovative future, importantly they could also effectively communicate that vision and inspire people around them. Mohammad Ali, Emmeline Pankhurst, Marie Curie, Steve Jobs and Nelson Mandela were all pioneers with a high level of Vision.

So, if Drive is the catalyst for seeking an outcome and Vision our ability to imagine what that could look and feel like, at this point the dopamine now flooding our brains means we are experiencing a degree of pleasure and reward that will help boost our motivation. We have lit the touch paper, and we are ready to set off on our endeavour.

BUT all the drive and vision in the world won't get us anywhere without the attribute of Self-efficacy: the belief in one's ability to get on and get it done.

"Vision without action is just a dream, action without vision just passes the time, but vision with action can change the world."

Nelson Mandela[19].

Self-efficacy
The belief in one's ability to achieve an outcome.

Self-efficacy describes our ability to achieve a goal or outcome despite it involving some kind of pain or discomfort. I score highly in my testing on self-efficacy and often describe it as the belief in my own 'personal power'. Now, it's worth mentioning, I fully accept that I am slightly deluded when it comes to this attribute, as I honestly believe I can do everything and anything. For example, I will be on my sofa at home watching a courtroom drama on TV with a glass of wine in one hand and a bag of snacks in the other. Halfway through the programme I'll turn to my wife and say, *"I would make a good defence barrister."* At which point, she would give me a wry smile and roll her eyes in pity. However, it's true, I honestly believe I would. Just like I also believe I could climb Everest on four months' notice or become the UK Prime Minister when I retire. These are not just flippant comments, in that moment I bloody mean it. Because I have an unbelievable belief in my ability to commit to something, work it out and succeed. Because my level of Self-efficacy is high.

Self-efficacy plays a huge role in our ability to push into High Road motivation and establish a Challenge State mindset. After all, if you believe you can do it, whether you're slightly deluded or not, then – guess what? You're already committed to giving it a go.

Here I should point out that to succeed in any endeavour, Self-efficacy requires a range of complementing characteristics, including Conscientiousness, Discipline and Resilience, but without doubt it's Self-efficacy that fires up our confidence.

While drive and vision create the spark and produce the dopamine to motivate us, Self-efficacy instils in us the belief that we can achieve our goal.

In his book *The Attributes: 25 Hidden Drivers of Optimal Performance* Rich Diviney comments, *"Self-efficacy can be dissected into components. It's a combination of confidence, initiative, and optimism. It's not just as simple as I've got this. That's just bravado. Self-efficacy is thoughtful and serious."*

I love this quote because Diviney underlines the fact that Self-efficacy is an attribute of serious thought and intent. Remember my sofa-induced pretensions to be a great defence barrister? Now, my level of Self-efficacy is possibly borderline delusional, I certainly know that it can appear that way to others, but it is never the case in my mind. I am deadly serious about my ability to take on challenges and succeed.

But not everyone is like this. Some people will be low and some moderate on Self-efficacy. Some people don't have a natural capacity to say to themselves, *"I can do this!"* and move forward with confidence. If you feel this describes you to a greater or lesser degree, there are some straightforward steps you can take to start practising and improving your Self-efficacy.

1. Challenge Staging – breaking down a challenge.

Challenge Staging is the process of breaking down a large, daunting task into smaller stages, enabling you to dip your toe in the water and test your level of confidence and competence before you commit yourself fully.

Imagine your challenge is to conquer your fear of heights. You decide that your goal is to jump off the ten-metre diving platform at the local swimming pool. Going straight up to the ten-metre platform is unrealistic. The fear will be overwhelming, propelling you immediately into Threat State, resulting in you retreating from the task and exacerbating your fear, whilst compromising your already low level of Self-efficacy.

Alternatively, if you decided to start with the three-metre springboard and practise three jumps from this height on your first visit to the pool, this would significantly increase your chances of success. You would be able to employ the visualisation and mental practice techniques we looked at earlier in the chapter, conquer this height and then move up in your mind to the next level with confidence and purpose.

On your next visit to the pool, you may move up to the five-metre platform and complete five jumps. Then the seven-metre platform and so on repeating the mental practice as you go. This represents what I call Challenge Staging. You are essentially breaking down a daunting and difficult challenge into smaller and more achievable chunks, gaining confidence at each stage. Yes, at some point you will have to go up to the ten-metre platform and, although it may still feel nerve wracking, the repetition you have gained from the staging exercise will have significantly increased your level of self-belief.

Another example could be that you decide you want to write a book. However, you have never performed well academically and, as you have low to moderate levels of Self-efficacy, you seriously doubt whether you have the literacy skills to pull it off. Using the Challenge Staging method, you start small. You begin writing a weekly blog and promote it on social media to practise your writing skills and gauge the reaction. You read books and materials similar to your style and follow other new authors to gain tips and techniques. Your blog appears to be well received, so you progress to writing the synopsis and content pages for your book. You share this with a few friends and family, again to gauge interest and the quality of content.

You then pluck up the courage to write the first chapter and share it with a professional editor who helps you review it for grammar and flow. The feedback through this process has been really positive and you are now starting to believe in yourself and find that you are ready to commit to completing your first book.

Challenge Staging is a great way to nudge your levels of Self-efficacy in the right direction. It may feel daunting to jump into something with both feet, so break it down, test the water and use visualisation. With every challenge you attempt and succeed in, your baseline levels of Self-efficacy will increase. This in turn means your self-belief and confidence to choose High Road motivation and push in to Challenge State will grow.

2. Challenge Observing – watching others take on difficult challenges.

Challenge Observing is the technique of seeking out and watching others who are taking on High Road and Challenge State situations. If you are low to moderate on Self-efficacy this can be a useful exercise, as it allows you to mentally assess whether you believe you can achieve or undertake the same challenge yourself. Obviously, this can go one of two ways: after observing others, you may think, *"That's not so bad, I could probably do that"* which helps programme positive thoughts and motivation in your mind. Or you may think, *"There is absolutely no way I could do that"* which could frame negative thoughts and demotivate you.

Whatever the outcome, both responses serve an important purpose when it comes to your Self-efficacy. Because it doesn't necessarily mean that you should be superbly confident in absolutely everything, sometimes it's about identifying the areas you want and need to be confident in. For every challenge you categorically rule out, there will be one or two that you choose to take on. So, Challenge Observing is a useful tool to identify what you would like to do versus what you really don't.

3. Challenge Statistics – programming the brain to rationalise risk.

As we have explored earlier in the book, our brain is primarily wired for survival, the first core function of human existence. This means that when it comes to taking on anything that remotely presents some risk, pain or discomfort, our brain naturally wants to talk us out of it. But we've also established that our ability to seek out and experience pleasure and reward relies on us taking on High Road motivation scenarios inducing a Challenge State of mind. So, if we are low to moderate on Self-efficacy, we may not have the confidence to challenge ourselves and reap the rewards we seek.

One of the best ways to increase confidence levels is to rationalise the challenge or situation as best we can. For example, you may have been terrified of flying for several years and, as a result, have avoided plane travel. Instead of sitting with your emotions and submitting to your survival instincts, you could quite easily research some official statistics about the relative safety of air travel.

Every year the International Civil Aviation Organization (ICAO) releases its global safety report. Their 2022 report revealed a 9.8% decrease in the global accident rate for 2021 versus 2020, meanwhile in 2021 fatalities fell by 66%[20]. Now, when you bear in mind that there were five fatal accidents among 32.2 million flights in 2022[21], this tells us that flying is one of the safest forms of travel in the world. Combine this with the fact that air safety continues to improve year on year, and you can start to rationalise that the fear you have around plane travel is completely out of kilter with the likelihood and reality of anything going wrong.

Studying facts and statistics around challenges and uncertainty can help us programme our brains to consider and interpret perceived risk in a more balanced and accurate way. This technique, although not solving the issue straight away, will begin to reduce the sensations of panic, enabling us to intercept the thoughts and feelings hijacking our levels of Self-efficacy around taking on an endeavour.

As we're discovering, Drive creates the desire, Vision allows us to foresee and get excited or daunted by the challenge ahead and Self-efficacy is the defining attribute that defines whether we can or cannot step up and say, *"I can do this."* So, we have started our business, we've written our book or we're on the runway ready to take off, we've made it this far. We're now going to need a couple of additional attributes to see the process through and reap the rewards our initial dopamine hit has promised us.

Accountability

Taking responsibility for, and ownership of, our decisions and actions.

If we are going to succeed in receiving pleasure and reward, Accountability is going to play an important role in what happens next.

Those of us who are willing to accept the consequences of our decisions and actions when things don't go well demonstrate high levels of Accountability. Likewise, those of us who blame others, our circumstances and environment demonstrate low levels of Accountability. Low accountability also significantly increases the chances of us giving up on our endeavour, as it's highly likely that we don't believe we can change our circumstances or influence the outcome. After all, it's not our fault, right?

Accountability is all about decisions and consequences. For example, if I decide to quit my job and start a business as a florist, then I've made a decision. The consequence of my decision is that it may not work out and I may become exposed financially and embarrassed personally. Initially, I've made my decision based on my **Drive** to succeed and better myself, I've then applied some **Vision** to foresee the benefits and rewards of making my business a success. I've clearly had enough **Self-efficacy** to back myself and push forward despite the risk and uncertainty. However, it's **Accountability** that I am going to need in abundance if I am not to falter at the first sign of difficulty and give up.

The first six months are tough, my start-up costs for supplies, materials and rent have exceeded my initial estimate and custom is slow, as I struggle to build my brand and credibility. To top it all off, we have just hit an economic downturn; inflation is high and consumer spending is down. In the absence of Accountability, I could easily give up, blame the economy, inflation and my landlord's unreasonable rent. I could talk myself into a position where it's not my fault, there is nothing I can do, so I just need to shut up shop, cut my losses and look for a new job.

Alternatively, with high levels of Accountability I am going to acknowledge that I am in this position because of the decisions I made and the risks I took. I'm likely to acknowledge that the economic situation isn't helping, but it's not insurmountable, after all there are plenty of other businesses in the same boat. This is going to push me to look around and seek solutions, not feel sorry for myself. Accountability is the attribute I'm leaning on here because it's my decisions, my responsibility and I am going to take ownership of my situation.

Here at T2, we work with organisations and teams on developing this as a key attribute for performance. In general, there are two types of Accountability:

- Accountability by Desire – I want to do this because there will be a reward.

- Accountability by Fear – I need to do this otherwise there will be consequences.

It doesn't really matter which of the two is the driving force, they should not be judged as either 'good' or 'bad', it very much depends on the person and the situation they find themselves in. Some people thrive on Accountability by Desire and are crippled by Accountability by Fear. Some are not motivated in the same way, as they need the prospect of discomfort to light a fire under them and that's OK. As long as Accountability is present, it's going to lead to higher degrees of personal ownership and responsibility, which in turn means greater staying power when the going gets tough. The key is learning which approach, Fear or Desire, you prefer and using that knowledge to keep yourself motivated and achieve the outcome you want.

Ultimately, when taking on High Road motivation situations and pushing yourself into Challenge State, Accountability is the attribute that will enable you to own your decisions, face up to any difficulties and force you in a direction that will lead to solutions and action. To do this effectively, however, you are going to need to be adaptable!

Adaptability
The ability to pivot, change or evolve.

Closing the circle of Drive, Vision, Self-efficacy and Accountability, the fifth and final attribute we require for seeking pleasure and reward is Adaptability.

Think back to Charles Darwin's 1859 work *On the Origin of Species* and his thoughts on genes being passed on to offspring enabling physical or behavioural adaptation that helped organisms better survive in their environment. Our entire existence has been built on our ability to adapt over hundreds of thousands of years and countless generations. However, the same concept serves us well in our everyday lives.

Every day, we all use our ability to adapt to changing circumstances and our environment. Some of us manage better than others. For those with low to moderate levels of Adaptability, life can be really challenging. In high-pressure situations it may even mean life or death. Here's my personal story of Adaptability...

In 2002 I was serving in the Royal Navy on board HMS Nottingham under Captain Richard Farrington. A highly experienced and respected leader, Farrington spent time building up strong relationships with the whole crew throughout our difficult and uncomfortable sea trials. A much anticipated seven-month tour to the Far East felt like the ship's reward. It was peacetime and four months in we arrived at Lord Howe Island in the Tasman Sea between Australia and New Zealand.

Five hundred miles from anywhere, the day was sunny. Ironically, the only reason we stopped and anchored off the island was because a member of the ship's company had injured their back and needed to be airlifted off the ship to be taken for treatment. Captain Farrington was paying a courtesy visit to the island's Mayor and had travel by helicopter whilst the ship was at anchor. Life was good. Suddenly, the weather rapidly began to change. The sea became rough, and the Command decided that the ship should weigh anchor and set out towards our next destination, Farrington agreed to finish up on the island and catch up with the ship using the helicopter.

The bridge team plotted the course and the ship picked up speed to 12 knots. Due to a series of decisions and events, the team had unintentionally plotted a course towards Wolf Rock. A large cluster of rocks surrounding Lord Howe Island, at low tide you can see it rising nine feet above the surface, at high tide however, Wolf Rock sits six feet beneath the waves, invisible.

HMS Nottingham hit Wolf Rock and ripped open a 160-foot (49-metre) hole in her hull below the waterline, as we were flung across the decks. Receiving the Mayday message whilst boarding the helicopter, once back on the bridge, with alarms going off and water pouring into her forward decks, Captain Farrington's first decision was to quieten the noise and restore some calm in order to think.

With the ship's bow wedged on the rock at the front, Farrington's first key decision was to reverse the ship off the rock to stop the force of the movement from the sea breaking the ship's spine. Once off the rock, water poured into the forward engine room too fast to recover the space and the hatches were closed on this and other affected decks.

With the ship's bow dipped dangerously low in the water, Farrington's second key decision was to purposely counter-flood the aft part of the ship. It felt counter-intuitive to flood an already sinking ship in rough seas but doing so, he reasoned, would stabilise her and give us time to pump out enough water to keep the ship afloat until we could receive help.

With the New Zealand Navy and Australian support potentially still hours away, the pressure of water in the compartment next to the aft engine room was buckling the bulkhead. Farrington knew that if that gave way, we would lose all power and with it our ability to use our pumps. If this happened the ship, in all likelihood would be lost. He also had in his mind the 250 sailors under his command.

His third key decision was to send me and three others to shore up the bulkhead in that aft engine room. At barely 19 years old, I *didn't hesitate because the confidence in my training and belief in Captain Farrington's leadership gave me the reassurance to crack on. We went down to the aft engine room and used everything we could lay our hands on to help shore up that bulkhead. It held for two hours, enough time to deploy further pumping equipment and keep the stricken ship afloat until we received support. It's a sore point but worth adding that not a week before, our rescuers were taking instruction from us, all serving to pile on the indignity of the situation.*

Captain Farrington's calm decision-making, our loyalty and his confidence in us drove our high-performance and efficiency. The whole ship's company contributed that evening and through Farrington's ability to adapt to a fast-changing situation and the crew's ability to work and adapt as a team, our lives and the ship were saved.

As the Captain, Farrington was on the hook for the whole disaster. He stood up and took full responsibility for the events that night. As a result he and three other senior officers were court-martialled and he never served at sea again. To those of us who served with him, he was and still is a hero. I'm still in touch with him today and he featured on our popular T2 podcast in 2023. He's a fantastic man to listen to.

Along with Captain Farrington's undoubted leadership qualities, it was his ability to adapt under extreme pressure that was critical. In turn, we as a team were able to show immense amounts of adaptability in a situation which was ever changing.

At T2 we put teams through our unique Pressure Rooms. These rooms are set up to deliver specific challenges. A team of five or six people enter the room and after a two-minute brief the clock starts. They have 20 minutes to complete their appointed task.

The tasks are carefully designed in such a way that the team is likely to make early mistakes and quickly realise that they need to try something different; they need to adapt what they are doing to make progress.

Amongst other attributes, we are testing for Adaptability: how quickly do the team work out that their early approach is suboptimal or simply not working. Secondly, how quickly do they react to this knowledge and adapt accordingly.

As you can imagine, some teams display high levels of Adaptability, while others continue to pursue their failing strategy throughout the duration of the task. We have captured and analysed the behaviour of teams with high Adaptability versus those with low Adaptability and here's what we've found: the teams who score high on Adaptability and perform well in our Pressure Rooms deploy three key high-performance techniques.

1. **Test & Review** – teams decide on an idea, test it and if it fails, they move on quickly.

2. **Open Gaze** – teams who take in their surroundings, check their environment and what's available to them, then factor this into their decision making.

3. **Marginal Gains Approach** – teams who change or improve their approach in small increments, based on what the last iteration of the process has taught them.

All these are techniques that individuals within their teams can learn and practise to improve their effectiveness and achieve greater levels of performance.

Just as we need a range of attributes and characteristics to endure pain and discomfort, which is important for our psychological balance, we also need to make sure we are seeking and experiencing pleasure and reward. To do this successfully and push into High Road motivation and Challenge State situations, we will need to draw on five important attributes.

We need **Drive**, which provides the need or desire to take on a challenge in the first place. We need **Vision** to bring the challenge and its potential rewards alive in our minds. We need **Self-efficacy** to provide us with the confidence and belief that we can step up and achieve the outcome. And, throughout the process we are going to need high levels of **Accountability** and **Adaptability** to navigate the challenges and difficulties we will face along the way.

The attributes and characteristics we have explored throughout Chapter 5 and 6 are all critical to our well-being and performance when we experience Threat or Challenge State situations. In Neutral State we don't really need high levels of anything, in fact we just need to sit nice and comfortably at baseline, giving ourselves time to recharge the mind and body.

Now that we have defined the characteristics and attributes for enduring pain and seeking pleasure, we're going to explore the fascinating interplay between the different generations we all represent. How do our generational differences contribute to our interpretation of, and ability to experience, pain and pleasure? With some key insights on the factors that have shifted over the past 70 years, it's time to mind the gap…

Chapter 7

Generational Shift
The time of our lives...

In this chapter we're going to explore how the era we're born in shapes our lives. A generation is defined as a group of individuals born within a specific span of time, or era, who share common knowledge and experiences. There are many factors which define the term generation, including genealogical, historical and sociological; however, in general, psychological researchers define a generation using a sociological approach. This approach is popular amongst psychological researchers because it highlights characteristics of each generation through people's experiences, values and attitudes.

The most popular sociological theory for defining generations is probably the generational cohort theory. Originating in the 1920s from Karl Mannheim's essay *The Problem of Generations* (translated in 1952)[22], generation cohort theory proposes that **social change and historical events during people's formative years leads to consistent patterns in thoughts, behaviours and values.** Today, Mannheim's work still influences psychological literature and is considered part of a wider field of psychological research, which explores individuals' understanding and interpretation of the world around them. Researchers' definitions of generational time periods can differ, give or take a few years, however, renowned generational expert Dr Alexis Abramson[23] defines them as:

- **The Silent Generation (1926–1945)**

- **Baby Boomers (1946–1964)**

- **Generation X (1965–1979)**

- **Generation Y or more popularly, Millennials (1980–1994)**

- **Generation Z (1995–2009)**

- **Generation Alpha (2010–2024)**

Generational definitions are most useful when they span a set age range, allowing us to draw meaningful comparisons. This is why recent generational definitions each span across a 15 year period. It follows that Generation Beta will span from 2025 to 2039.

Let's now explore each generation. Starting in 1926, we're going to look at how generational experiences and influences may have helped shape those individuals' relationship with pain and pleasure; how their nurture and world view has been impacted by their environment, historical events and the cultural shifts they lived through. Will you recognise your parents and early influencers? Might you recognise yourself, your siblings and close friends? How about your children or young adults close to you?

It's worth noting that not every single person who was born within these generational time periods will behave and respond to situations in the same way. After all, we have already explored how unique our individual personalities and world views are. However, we do know that each generation has experienced the same consistent influences and, therefore, we must consider these when looking at our relationship with pain and pleasure. For our purposes we begin in 1926. Prior to 1926 are the Greatest Generation and, prior to 1900, the Lost Generation. The following research and data have primarily been taken from UK and US studies and reflect generational shifts within these cultures and demographics.

The Silent Generation   1926–1945

Our first defined generational group. These are people who were born during or lived through World War II and the Great Depression. The name Silent Generation comes from an article in *Time Magazine* from the 1950s, and alludes to the fact that, as children, they were taught to be "seen and not heard". According to Dr Abramson, their behavioural similarities include being:

- **Disciplined and cautious**

- **Value-orientated and loyal**

- **Hard-working**

- **Resilient and determined**

Parental Influence
Members of this generation are known for working within the system rather than fighting against it. By and large they were brought up to comply, and their own parenting styles were centred around compliance and discretion. Children were to be seen and not heard. This generation contained some of the youngest parents of all generations and, as a result, were likely to still be being parented with expectation and discipline by their own parents. This would have led to a lot of mirroring in their own parenting style.

Social Influence
Experiencing a lot of challenge and adversity in their early years running up to parenthood, the Silent Generation endured a world war; the fall of the Nazis; the rise of the nuclear bomb; the Great Depression following the US stock market crash in 1929 and scarcity. As a result, many were raised, educated and influenced to seek financial security and stability. A strong work ethic was incredibly high amongst this group, as their experiences of hardship drove them to provide at all costs.

Educational Influence

Research today suggests that the more recent generations are better educated than the Silent Generation for a number of reasons; including the following:

Marriage: early marriages meant fewer young adults moving onto further education.

Children: earlier marriage meant children came along sooner and in higher numbers than modern-day generations. The average number of children per family in the UK in 1948 was 2.19, compared to 2018 where it drops to 1.89[24].

Education: only 9% of the Silent Generation was awarded a degree-level qualification before the age of 36, compared to 36% of Millennials[25].

The Workplace: as a result of war and economic depression, the Silent Generation grew up with scarcity. They were more likely to enter the workplace to start earning and providing earlier in life, reducing their choices when it came to work versus further education.

The Silent Generation's World

Cultural and social influences, combined with first-hand experiences of war and severe economic recession contributed to a general sense of patriotism and the desire for security and stability. Hardship and scarcity meant that the Silent Generation generally handled money and finances with care and discretion. They were taught to collaborate with others and show respect to those in authority, meaning they were well equipped to forge positive workplace relationships and fit into hierarchies.

Parenting styles and societal experiences meant that the Silent Generation became incredibly determined and resilient; persevering through adversity and bouncing back from failures and challenges.

The saying, *"They don't make them like they used to!"* is usually used to describe the Silent Generation, because their courage, bravery and relentless determination was their greatest asset.

The Silent Generation possessed the ability to endure pain and discomfort to a greater degree than some of the more recent generations. However, because of their cautious approach to risk, finances and societal expectations around conformity, the likelihood of them pushing into Challenge State scenarios and expressing themselves creatively or freely would not be as high as with generations to come. Yet, moving into a post-war world, the Silent Generation's children are boosting the population and their parental influence will become key to the next phase of societal transformation.

Baby Boomers   1946–1964

As you might expect, Baby Boomers are named after the spike in births at the end of World War II. "Boomers" are the children of the resilient, robust, respectful and cautious Silent Generation with many historians attributing the birth rate phenomenon to a sense of optimism for the future, a more positive economic outlook and those couples who had put off having children in the war years all starting to conceive at the same time. The group starts around 1946 and ends with those born around 1964, when the birthrate began to decline again. In general terms, Dr Abramson describes Boomers as:

- **Committed and hard-working:** a mirror trait instilled in them by their parents.

- **Self-sufficient:** given much more childhood freedom than their parents.

- **Competitive:** due to sheer numbers of other children in neighbourhoods and schools.

- **Social skills:** pre-technological revolution so had to develop strong social skills.

- **Ambitious:** growing post-war optimism in industry and economic potential.

- **Digital immigrants:** born when telephones and televisions were the newest technological household items, as opposed to being 'digital natives' like more recent generations.

Parental Influence

Baby Boomers started to engage with their children in a more focused way, putting greater emphasis on education. Coming into and living through a post-war, more optimistic and liberal time, more in touch with their fun and expressive side, they encouraged their children to do the same (think Summer of Love in 1967[26]). Although there was still a level of discipline and rigour around rules and education, parenting was more of a two-way dialogue rather than a directive parent-child relationship.

Boomers were the first generation to bring in family meetings and encourage input from children. Yet, Boomers were, and still are to date, the generation that saw the highest divorce rate, with a noticeable spike in the 1980s and 90s, meaning many children of this generation experienced high levels of parental discord and separation. This, without question, plays a role in future generations' attitude to their relationships and parenting styles.

Social Influence

Boomers were the beneficiaries of both the post-war housing revolution and better healthcare provision. Most would have been born in rented accommodation, particularly in densely populated urban areas, much of which was likely to have been in urgent need of renewal. In 1950 only one in four people owned their own home, by 1970 it was one in three and by the mid 1980s, just 35 years later, two out of three, or two-thirds of working people owned their own homes[27]. Alongside home ownership, affordable package holidays abroad, rising incomes and higher standards of living, Boomers' ambitions and expectations grew. This led to a different attitude to risk and a more expansive, idealistic approach to their life choices compared to the generation before.

Educational Influence

Baby Boomers experienced greater levels of education to that of the previous generation. For example, in the US nearly 89% of Boomers completed high school, of which 28.5% would go on to hold a degree-level qualification or higher. Back in the UK, those who completed a degree-level education or higher was 16%, almost double that of the Silent Generation[28].

The Baby Boomers' World

Baby Boomers were born and lived in a time that saw a massive shift from war and economic hardship to peace, optimism and prosperity. They benefited from increased quality and accessibility to healthcare, education, travel and home ownership, so their attitude to the art of what's possible shifted. As a result, they became less risk averse and more ambitious about the future with high expectations for their standards of living.

Boomers did, however, retain some of the values and characteristics of the Silent Generation when it came to education, discipline and work ethic. It's therefore reasonable to suggest that this generation had a relatively strong ability to endure pain and discomfort carried over from their parents' and grandparents' influence. The greatest shift for this generation was in their desire (and ability) to seek out pleasure and reward. With greater prospects economically, financially and societally, Boomers started to take more risks which translated into significant improvement and advances in industry, employment, science and technology.

Generation X 1965–1979

Born between 1965 and 1979, Generation X represents the children of both late Silent Generation parents and the Baby Boomers. Often referred to as the 'latchkey generation', 'Gen Xers' were more likely to be left home alone because both parents were out at work. This phenomenon directly correlates with the statistics around an increase of women entering the workplace, combined with the presence of more single mums due to the significant increase in the Baby Boomer divorce rates. With the first moon landing in 1969, Gen Xers were growing up in a time of accelerated technological advancements but with personal access still not as readily available as it is today. With an understanding of the importance of both the non-digital and digital world, this generation also saw a significant increase in access to TV, entertainment and gaming. Dr Abramson describes Generation X as being:

- **Resourceful:** due to economic uncertainty.

- **Logical:** good problem solvers.

- **Independent:** with greater levels of freedom as children.

- **Work-life balance orientated:** the first generation to really value levels of flexibility and consider mental health more broadly.

- **Digitally diverse:** with a strong technological capability, due to growing up in a world of rapidly changing technology.

Parental Influence
Although marriage rates were lower for Gen X than for our Baby Boomers, when they did get married, they stayed married at much higher rates and started to place a higher value on work-life balance with both mum and dad active in the workplace. Children of late Boomers and early Gen Xers were offered even more levels of freedom, often playing out until the street lights came on. Although technology and gaming were both now evolving quickly,

it was still early days in mass adoption and children of early Gen Xers still spent a lot of time outdoors.

Social Influence

Generally, Generation X children grew up in a time when there were more dual-income or single-parent families, meaning this generation spent a lot of time fending for themselves. This, in turn, instilled independence and self-efficacy. They were also the first generation to grow up with the advent of personal computing, cable television and MTV, and were heavily influenced by music and fashion. Despite this opening up of the world, shaky economic conditions, job losses and recessions during the 70s and 80s meant that Gen Xers had to learn to be resourceful in their childhood and adolescent years. They also had to learn to develop greater levels of resilience, as in 1989 Britain, Europe and the US faced their first pandemic since Spanish Flu in 1919: the HIV/AIDS pandemic[29].

Educational Influence

Continued economic instability and the end of free higher education in the UK in the late 90s meant that Gen Xers racked up more student debt than any previous generation, which would take them decades to pay off. Those who decided to skip an expensive education entered the job market on the heels of a recession and, as a result, many found themselves either unemployed or underemployed. Now adults, they earned the name "Boomerang Kids" because, of those that had left home to study, many had no choice but to move back in with their parents or family members, job hunting with little prospect of buying or renting their own home.

Generation X's World

Born between the transformational time of the Baby Boomers and more notable Millennials, Generation X is often overlooked. Following the optimism and growth of the early Boomer years, Gen Xers were given unprecedented amounts of freedom, resulting in independence and resourcefulness. Again, like Boomers, Gen Xers are also referred to as digital immigrants accessing the growing availability of personal computers and mobile phones. However, although they didn't experience the hardship of war or the Great Depression, they certainly didn't have it all their own way. Times were tough financially; they endured boom and bust economics and expensive higher education.

Most had reached late teenage years or early adulthood by the 90s, which saw them carry over some traits and characteristics to endure a level pain and discomfort, but probably not to the levels previous generations had become accustomed to. They did, after all, grow up with a level of comfort and provision greater than that of previous generations. When it came to seeking pleasure and reward, whereas Boomers were labelled "workaholics", Gen Xers were labelled "slackers", both unfair labels for two entire generations, but in general this reflected the environments they grew up in, the levels of optimism, opportunity and the slight differences in characteristics and traits that emerged.

Generation Y, the Millennials   1980–1994

Representing those born between 1980 and 1994, this is the cohort you may have heard about most. Often labelled "lazy", Millennials are the first generation to be true "digital natives". There's also a distinction made between early Millennials and their late Millennial counterparts, as societal and cultural change during this 15-year period were more rapid and transformative than for any previous generation. For example, if you were born in 1980 to Baby Boomer parents, then the early part of your childhood would be more closely aligned with that of the previous generation, whereas, if you were born in 1994 to Generation X parents, your early influences and environment was likely to be very different.

The pace of change from 1980–2020 technologically, economically and educationally was unprecedented, which has meant that Millennials in particular offer us fewer common trends. However, what research we do have highlights some patterns and defining characteristics of Millennials, including:

- **Self-sufficiency:** no longer relying on others to solve their problems or teach them things; they have the Internet for that.

- **Confidence and curiosity:** encouraged to speak up more than any other generation.

- **Sceptical of authority:** more likely to question authority. Abramson notes this could offend older generations less likely to behave in that way.

- **Digital immigrants shifting to natives:** communicating predominantly via the Internet, on social media and on mobile phones.

- **Importance of education:** typically have higher expectations, societally and individually around education.

- **Holding high expectations of living standards**

- **Purpose versus necessity:** more likely to do what they want, not just what they need.

Parental Influence

As they reached adulthood, Millennials are the first parental generation we can clearly see having fewer children. Not only this, but marriage rates drop significantly with more children being born out of wedlock. Rebelling slightly from the parental experiences of their childhood, Millennial parents tend to focus less on discipline and reprimand and more on open-mindedness and reinforcement. They encourage their children to be authentic and have their own opinions. There is a question around how effective this type of parental approach is. Are we seeing children and teenagers of Millennial's displaying less discipline, a lack of boundaries and a reduced respect for authority? Is the elevated empowerment around reinforcement, identity and purpose out of kilter? This area of research is currently being debated. There is no doubt, however, that children of Millennials are surrounded by resource and abundance and are more likely to have experienced foreign travel, spacious houses, the latest technology and material possessions.

Social Influence

Millennials grew up in the age of the Internet, widely available personal computing and mobile phone technology. Early Millennials' life experiences are more aligned with the digital immigrants of Generation X, whereas later Millennials are considered the first true digital natives, in that they have not experienced a world without it. However, Millennials have been labelled the "Unluckiest Generation" because they have experienced slower economic growth since entering the workplace than any other generation before them.

The emergence of the digital world, things such as online gaming, social media and dating sites, has produced significant shifts in the time people spend outdoors versus indoors, together with the number of young people socialising, dating and even having sex. Housing markets too have been more challenging for late Millennials, with house prices rising to unachievably high levels for many first-time buyers, also paving the way for a rise in foreclosures, evictions and job losses following the 2008 financial crisis.

Educational Influence

Research shows that despite the economic turbulence and the rising costs of going on to further education, statistically, Millennials are more educated than any previous generation. In the UK, a staggering 40% of Millennials have a university degree[30]. But with an uncertain employment market, many highly qualified Millennials still find it difficult to enter careers with the pay and prospects they desire.

Millennials' World

As of writing this book in 2024, now aged between 30 and 45 years old, at around 40% Millennials currently represent the largest group in the workplace. Since 2000 we have seen the biggest shift in people's attitudes to work and workplace culture, societal expectations around diversity, inclusion and overall expectations around standards of living. Combine this with accelerating advances in digital capability and accessibility, and you can see why Millennials' attitude and behaviour tends to dominate the conversation.

While Boomers and Gen Xers may say of our largely Millennial-led world that, *"We have lost our way and don't have the resilience, grit and discipline we once had"*, Millennials and younger generations can equally counter this with, *"Thank goodness we have evolved!"* Either way, when it comes to enduring pain and seeking pleasure, there is no doubt that something within our society's attitude, behaviour and values has significantly shifted. A shift that is producing some concerning statistics.

Poor mental health has risen significantly in Millennials and Generation Z compared to that of previous generations. In a 2018 American Psychological Association (APA) survey, only 56% of Millennials said that they had good to excellent mental health. Compare that to Baby Boomers who reported 70% good mental health and the stalwart Silent Generation coming in at 74%[31]. In addition, according to the American medical insurance company, Blue Cross Blue Shield Association, the diagnosis of major depression in the US is increasing more quickly among Millennials and Generation Z than any other generation[32] and UK figures show a similar trajectory.

Despite up to five generations all co-existing in our society in 2024, in the same environment with similar influences and challenges, it is Millennials and Generation Z that seem to be struggling to endure pain and discomfort the most. There are lots of theories around why this may be, but as we explored earlier in the book, the pain-pleasure scales are out of balance, the comfort crisis is real and the way the human brain is responding to this is, without doubt, a contributing factor. Given the issues Generation Z are experiencing today, let's now take a look at this group.

Generation Z   1995–2009

Early "Gen Zs" are now in their 20s and already impacting society, the world and workplace. Born in 1995 up to 2009, this group is still very young and has never known a life without technology. Their alternative name, coined by American psychologist Dr Jean Twenge, is the Internet Generation or iGen. Some of their generational characteristics include:

- **A love of exploration and travel.**

- **Superior digital and technological capability:** these are digital natives with high degrees of dexterity.

- **Ambitious and money driven:** financial security is important to them.

- **Diversity of employment:** an expanding choice of work, thanks to the digital revolution and ability to work remotely, as well as on-site.

- **Self-care:** they seek assurance for their health and the future; changes in the Earth's climate and experience of the COVID-19 pandemic have made them politically progressive.

- **Sensitivity:** more prone to anxiety than previous generations.

- **Cognitive evolution:** research suggests that Gen Z brains show structural differences to those of earlier generations. In Darla Rothman's 2016 essay *A Tsunami of Learners Called Generation Z*[33], she proposes these differences are the effect of the way the brain responds to its immediate environment. Gen Z brains are wired to engage with sophisticated, complex visual imagery like that on smartphones and tablets, which they have always been exposed to. As a result, the visual part of their brains is far more developed, making their learning via visual methods much more effective in comparison to auditory methods, such as discussion and lecture formats.

Parental Influence

There is no extensive research yet, however early data suggests that late Millennial and early Gen Z parents are rewriting the rules of parenting. They seem more determined than previous generations to be different, demonstrating even higher degrees of freedom and trust with their children; becoming far more inclusive in allowing their children to make their own decisions, adopting a "parenting is a complement, not a compromise" approach. When it comes to boundaries and discipline, Gen Z parents are generally siding on the reinforcement of positive behaviours and encouraging the exploration of personal values, beliefs and identities, rather than reprimanding negative behaviours and the enforcement of their parental values and beliefs.

The one area in which late Millennial and Gen Z parents appear to differ is digital adoption and use. Some believe it's the world they're growing up in and it's inevitable, so let children dictate their own routines and boundaries. Some believe it's damaging and are trying to establish ground rules when it comes to time and energy spent purely on computers, gaming, mobile phones and social media. Either way, we are, quite possibly, watching the most empowered generation of children the world has ever seen grow up. What that may mean for the future we will explore later in the book.

Social Influence

Generation Z are growing up in a society richer in instantly available information than ever before. Top of the list in terms of influence and impact on their identities and view of the world are:

- **Politics:** they're becoming more politically progressive than previous generations; socialism versus capitalism, climate, health and world conflict are important to Gen Zs, as are issues around 'fake news' and the rise of artificial intelligence.

- **Mental health:** with increasing rates of poor mental health, Gen Zs are more likely to do something about it than previous generations.

- **Equality, diversity and inclusion:** well-educated on historic events, identity issues and cultures, through a period of rising tensions, Gen Zs are determined to change the world.

- **Money:** anxious about their ability to afford housing, the cost of living and future sustainability of industries, jobs and lifestyles.

- **Socialising and relationships:** able to operate their entire social life digitally, from chatting with friends to dating, everything can be done online. But not everything and that could be a problem.

Educational Influence

Without question, Generation Z has been afforded the greatest levels of education, and improved education is the one consistently upward trend since the Silent Generation. Not only are schools, colleges and universities more accessible and progressive, but their ability to supercharge their general education using technology has seen them become more connected and collaborative with their learning than ever before. They have benefited from a true blended learning approach which has seen greater levels of engagement. However, the impact of the COVID-19 pandemic in 2020 and 2021, resulting in interrupted and inconsistent secondary and higher education, will likely emerge as this group makes its way into adulthood.

Generation Z's world

Forbes magazine stated Gen Zs "... are set to become Generation Smart". In a study 89% of Gen Zs think that a college or university education is valuable[34]. With unprecedented access to knowledge and information at such an early stage of brain development, the opposing argument is how detrimental this may be in shaping certain thoughts and beliefs, and how free are they to apply critical thinking if all they need to do is type or ask a question of a search engine or chatbot? Artificial intelligence will also make its mark on Gen Z; their education and world of work changing faster than at any other time as technology and its application directs and defines more and more of our daily lives. From environmental breakdown and the polarisation of political thought to the proliferation of "fake news", Gen Zs want stability and are yearning for trust.

Research is also emerging that Generation Z engages in significantly lower sexual activity before the age of 25 than previous generations, coinciding with a rise in poor mental health[35]. There are multiple studies underway around why this may be with many theories emerging. Is it the availability and accessibility of online pornography diluting their experiences and understanding of intimacy? We touched on this in Chapter 2 with Dr Anna Lembke's work exploring the science behind addiction and how dopamine works with respect to addictive online behaviours. Could it be down to higher rates of anxiety and depression? Or is it as simple as Gen Zs don't socialise face-to-face in pubs and clubs as much as previous generations? Whatever's going on, the concern for the future could be that less serious relationships means less sex and less sex means less babies, and less babies... Well, that will create a population, production and provision problem in 40 to 50 years from now!

Let's look back for a moment and chart our progress from the stoic values of the highly resilient Silent Generation to the Boomers who took the hard working ethics of their parents and benefited from the post-war bounce in prosperity and ambition; Generation X who saw tough times but navigated it with a fair amount of balance and self-reliance; Millennial parents becoming more engaged with their children saw huge shifts in their lives by the exponentially increasing impact of the digital world and declining mental health of Gen Z set against a backdrop of tough economics, world conflict, environmental breakdown and cultural division. So who's next?

Generation Alpha   2010–2024

The next generation has been dubbed Generation Alpha by social researcher Mark McCrindle. Whilst not specialising in this group, Dr Abramson predicts that these children, the majority of which are the offspring of highly engaged Millennials, will be family-orientated and more digitally savvy than any previous generation. She also thinks this might be a cohort where generational labels start to lose some of their usefulness because, as more than 2.8 million humans are born globally every week, Gen Alpha's predicted head count will reach nearly two billion, the largest generation in the history of the world.

It's predicted that Gen Alpha will also benefit from the greatest material wealth, be the most technologically savvy and, due to advanced technology and healthcare, live the longest. Gen Alpha will also remain in education longer and are predicted to live at home well into their late 20s, giving their parents an extended parental role. The early developmental cost of enforced home education and loss of social interaction during 2020 and 2021 due to COVID-19 restrictions will also become more apparent as these children grow up and enter adulthood, as will access to and navigation of the digital world with use of smartphones in younger and younger children. It is hard to predict the economic and societal influences for this large cohort, however the climate, culture and world conflict is likely to play a consistent role throughout their early years.

Generational shift over the last 100 years provides us with a chronological timeline of parental, social and educational evolution. Although we are all primarily wired by the three core functions of existence – survival, reproduction and purpose – we form our main characteristics, attributes and personality styles from our nature, nurture and view of the world. You can now also see how our nurture and overall view of the world is heavily influenced by the generation into which we were born. What was going on around us in our formative years plays a huge role in our relationship with pain and pleasure, and ultimately impacts our world view.

Now that we have explored which generation we belong to and the broad ramifications of that experience, and added it to the information we have uncovered about ourselves through our earlier testing, let's head back and revisit our world view again…

The question is, are you happy with your world view?

Is it serving you well?

Is it holding you back?

More importantly, is there an opportunity for you to challenge or modify it?

It's time to open your mind and find some marginal gains to help you balance your relationship with pain and pleasure.

Chapter 8

Your World View Revisited

Is it serving you well?

We previously explored the inner workings of your World View in Chapter 4. Now, having weighed up our generational influences, it's worth revisiting this. A 'personal compass', our world view plays a powerful role in how we endure pain and experience pleasure. Let's quickly review the beliefs that make up our world view and ask ourselves some questions: Is my world view serving me well? Which elements may be holding me back? And how might this cause my pain-pleasure scales to tip out of balance?

To briefly recap, our world view has two distinct parts:

- **Our current, mental model of how the world is organised, structured and operates.**

- **How much, or how little, we buy into or agree with that framework.**

Remember, our world view matters because it feeds into our ability to endure pain and uncertainty in **Threat State**, seek pleasure and reward in **Challenge State** or just rest and recuperate in **Neutral State**.

Different for each of us, our world view is generally formed by our response to the five key questions that follow:

Take time to review your World View test results from Chapter 4 or, alternatively, if you haven't taken the free T2 based World View test yet, simply answer the following questions with a short sentence or paragraph. If you want to move ahead and return to this section later, turn to page 128 and continue with The Power of Control.

1.	How do I believe the world was created? Our religious or scientific position.
2.	How do I believe the world operates? Our political, societal, environmental position.
3.	Do I agree with or accept how the world operates? Our acceptance position.
4.	What are my motivations and values? Our morale position.
5.	What happens to us when we die? Our spiritual or evolutionary position.

Using your answers to these key five questions, now try to decide which of the following elements, contribute to your world view.

Humanism: the world is a natural place based on science and reason.

1. When does this belief serve me well?

2. When does this belief hold me back?

3. What are the warning signs to watch out for with this belief?

4. If you were to question this belief, what questions would you ask?

Pantheism: the world was created by God or a supreme entity.

1. When does this belief serve me well?

2. When does this belief hold me back?

3. What are the warning signs to watch out for with this belief?

4. If you were to question this belief, what questions would you ask?

Optimism: the world is my oyster; hope is key, and anything is possible.

1. When does this belief serve me well?

2. When does this belief hold me back?

3. What are the warning signs to watch out for with this belief?

4. If you were to question this belief, what questions would you ask?

Pessimism: the world is corrupt; I trust very few people.

1. When does this belief serve me well?

2. When does this belief hold me back?

3. What are the warning signs to watch out for with this belief?

4. If you were to question this belief, what questions would you ask?

Moralism: the world should be fair and just; we should share the same morals and values.

1. When does this belief serve me well?

2. When does this belief hold me back?

3. What are the warning signs to watch out for with this belief?

4. If you were to question this belief, what questions would you ask?

Moral Subjectivism: the world is morally indifferent; morals and values are all subjective.

1. When does this belief serve me well?

2. When does this belief hold me back?

3. What are the warning signs to watch out for with this belief?

4. If you were to question this belief, what questions would you ask?

Individualism: I will control my own destiny; I will be self-reliant and make my own success.

1. When does this belief serve me well?

2. When does this belief hold me back?

3. What are the warning signs to watch out for with this belief?

4. If you were to question this belief, what questions would you ask?

Collectivism: things should be done together and for the greater good of all.

1. When does this belief serve me well?

2. When does this belief hold me back?

3. What are the warning signs to watch out for with this belief?

4. If you were to question this belief, what questions would you ask?

Stoicism: I must be strong and endure the pain and challenge of life.

1. When does this belief serve me well?

2. When does this belief hold me back?

3. What are the warning signs to watch out for with this belief?

4. If you were to question this belief, what questions would you ask?

Entitleism: I deserve to have what I want. I deserve pleasure, reward and happiness.

1. When does this belief serve me well?

2. When does this belief hold me back?

3. What are the warning signs to watch out for with this belief?

4. If you were to question this belief, what questions would you ask?

Feel free to take a moment and check back with the examples I gave in Chapter 4 about Sarah and John, and how the elements identified by our questions informed their world view.

Keep your responses in mind because we'll shortly be returning to them. First, it's important to understand why this deep dive into our world view is crucial and how we can refine, enhance and adapt it.

The Power of Control

When it comes to performance psychology, one of the most influential techniques we teach here at T2, whether that be to senior corporate executives, elite sports athletes or in general 1-2-1 coaching sessions, is the power of control.

As we have discovered, we humans feel most comfortable in a state of relaxation, because, quite often, this **Neutral State** is where we feel a sense of complete control: our survival instinct is not activated; we are not stressed or stretched in terms of challenge or uncertainty; and so we exist comfortably, expending little effort and experiencing little concern.

Threat State is the state in which we, without question, feel the most out of control. If something happens in our physical environment or we experience a negative thought that could result in damaging consequences for us, then we can quickly feel threatened, worried or anxious. Ultimately, we experience the sensation of being out of control, which leads to a damaging and self-perpetuating cycle of Threat State.

The same can happen in **Challenge State** situations, albeit with less impact if we have chosen to push into Challenge State. This is because we feel a greater degree of control due to know-how, experience or prior preparation. However, it would be safe to say that we won't feel totally in control, especially if the challenge carries uncertainty or risk.

Fundamentally, it is our ability to wrestle back control physically and mentally that will determine how successful we are at navigating Threat and Challenge State situations.

Having the ability to quickly identify what we can or can't control by way of action, thought or belief, is incredibly important.

Controllables vs Non-controllables

Let's now look back at your World View results, or the answers you gave to the five questions I posed earlier in this chapter. Think about the elements and beliefs that you have a higher degree of control over, versus the ones you don't. If we're going to take more control over our lives, we must first make sure we stand a fighting chance of doing so. To help you better understand this we need to define the difference between an **Internal and External Locus of Control**.

Internal Locus of Control – you believe that you are in control of your life and possess the ability to operate within the world based on your decisions and actions. You therefore attribute your success or failure to your own efforts and abilities.

External Locus of Control – you believe that you are not in control of your life and are largely governed by your environment and circumstance. You attribute your success or failure to external factors outside your control, such as luck or fate.

It simply comes down to this. Are you empowered or limited by your beliefs?

For example, one element of my world view is **Individualism**. This belief has an internal locus of control, meaning that no matter what is happening in the world around me or what other people think, feel or do, I believe that I control how I act and react. The power, therefore, to make decisions and act is always in my own hands.

So, Individualism comes with a high degree of control. The trade-off, however, is that selfish behaviour could creep in if my Individualism is too dominant: if I don't think about others and the impact of my actions upon them. However, in the main, Individualism serves me well because it gives me a high degree of control over my thoughts, actions and reactions. It gives me the sense that I am only ever one decision away from dealing with a problem. No belief is inherently either 'good' or 'bad' unless it becomes extreme,

The opposing belief to Individualism is **Collectivism**, which is the belief that things should be done together and for the greater good of all. Now, this is a wonderfully virtuous human belief, and if you have this there are many ways in which this will serve you well. However, this belief has an external locus of control, meaning that for Collectivism to become a reality, you require external forces outside your control to align, in order for it to be effective. For this reason Collectivism has a greater potential to put you into Threat State because your personal element of control is low. It could, therefore, cause you more frustration than fulfilment, as the lack of Collectivism you experience from others sabotages your belief system time and again.

I'm not saying that Collectivism should not form part of your world view, on the contrary, it's an element that has achieved many important progressive actions throughout human history, but … **if your world view is going to serve you well, you need to ensure that overall, it has a balanced degree of elements and beliefs with an internal locus of control for personal empowerment.** If not, you could very quickly end up feeling out of control and frustrated. Indeed, a lot of people I coach discover that most of the elements of their world view are external locus of control, which has led to a rise in frustration and a downward spiral of self-worth.

I feel I need to mention here **Idealism and Realism**. As you can imagine, they are closely related to Collectivism and Individualism and when describing a persons value system we often use these terms. Idealism is what's in our minds: a high-minded or noble pursuit – whereas Realism is a response to life as it really is – unfiltered fact. Collectivism promotes the common good with high ideals for betterment: it has, therefore, a degree of Idealism. Individualism and an individual's ability to make change is rooted more in Realism and focuses us on dealing with how the world really operates. A combination of these elements creates a powerful engine for change.

"Never doubt that a small group of thoughtful, committed citizens can change the world; indeed, it's the only thing that ever has."

Margaret Mead[36]

So the key to a balanced world view is not to have an extreme or overly high internal or external locus of control. Here are two examples of extreme world view combinations that would constitute high internal versus high external locus of control.

Someone with an extreme world view with a high internal locus of control would display elements such as: **Optimism, Moral Subjectivism, Individualism and Stoicism**.

Someone with an extreme world view with a high external locus of control would display elements such as: **Pessimism, Moralism, Collectivism and Entitleism**.

Your world view combinations probably won't align with the extreme examples I've just given and hopefully you have a blend of internal and external locus of control.

Pause here and carry out a quick tick box exercise of your world view beliefs below:

Internal Locus of Control

☐ Individualism & Realism

☐ Optimism

☐ Moral Subjectivism

☐ Stoicism

External Locus of Control

☐ Collectivism & Idealism

☐ Pessimism

☐ Moralism

☐ Entitleism

Take time to reflect on these outcomes and your World View test results or the questions you answered at the beginning of this chapter.

- What beliefs present the greatest opportunity for you to enhance your world view or make it work better for you today?

- How can you maintain your world view but take back more control so that it doesn't frustrate or inhibit you?

Misinformation and Disinformation

How the modern-day world influences and reinforces our internal narratives.

In the final section of this chapter, and before we move onto how we balance the scales for greater mental and psychological well-being, we're going to highlight the growing influence of misinformation and disinformation. We will explore the difference between them, their impact on our world view and why, as a result, societies around the world are becoming more polarised or divided than ever before.

Misinformation – false or inaccurate information due to flawed research, unsubstantiated facts, unreliable or unverified sources.

Disinformation – false or inaccurate information created or curated specifically to deliberately deceive.

Although one appears more sinister and indeed criminal than the other, both misinformation and disinformation have the same effect: they deliver false or misleading information about a person, situation or circumstance, leading to an incorrect narrative or opinion forming in our minds. Continual consumption of such mis or disinformation means that these narratives and opinions are reinforced, becoming stronger and more deep seated.

The digital and online world we live in today only serves to amplify the reach of mis and disinformation. Let's talk conspiracy theories... For example, it has been claimed that 5G cellular networks cause cancer because 5G radio waves are supposedly harmful to human cells and tissues. Medical experts have debunked these claims many times, explaining that 5G radio waves cannot damage or alter the DNA in our cells, in fact they cannot even penetrate our skin[37]. The 5G cancer scare is misinformation because it is factually and scientifically incorrect. However, millions of people have read this misinformation repeatedly online for the past few years with the result being that many have developed a deep-seated belief that 5G can induce cancer.

From a notorious and highly damaging piece of disinformation, the vaccination rate of children around the world has dipped for the combined MMR vaccine that prevents the serious illnesses measles, mumps and rubella. Alarm bells are ringing in public health circles due to a rise in outbreaks of these life-threatening diseases. The drop-off in infant vaccination can be traced back to the late 1980s and an article published in a respected English medical journal. Gastroenterologist Dr Andrew Wakefield and 12 colleagues claimed that the use of the MMR vaccine may predispose children to developing autism.

On investigation, it was found that Wakefield and his colleagues falsified facts and figures for financial gain[38]. Disgraced, Wakefield was struck off the medical register in the UK, and although debunked many times by experts and organisations over the following years, many concerned parents stopped taking their children to be vaccinated and the impact of Wakefield's disinformation persists today.

These types of incidents create an increasing degree of fear and mistrust in scientific research, established organisations and civil society, and before you know it, climate change is a hoax, the COVID-19 pandemic was staged, 9/11 was an inside job and the moon landings never happened.

Misinformation and disinformation for me presents one of the greatest threats to human existence, and before you roll your eyes at that statement, let me explain why.

Over the years scientists have pondered the possible events and circumstances that could wipe out our species. These are known as existential threats and, in general, it's considered there are five main threats:

1. **Ecological Breakdown** – lack of biodiversity, climate change, breakdown in Earth's ecosystem.

2. **Nuclear War** – the destruction of life.

3. **Mass Extinction Event** – an unforeseen once-in-a-50-million-year event such as a large asteroid or meteor strike.

4. **Widespread Disease** – a deadly pandemic for which we find no cure.

5. **Artificial Intelligence** – AI-induced breakdown or overhaul of society.

Due to human ingenuity and our ability to problem solve, adapt and overcome, these existential threats are unlikely to happen any time soon. However, it is misinformation and disinformation that could well prevent us from addressing immediate – or avoiding future – catastrophe.

The unprecedented rise of mis and disinformation and its ability to swiftly spread via social media and the Internet, combined with algorithmic bias and flawed AI, means we have already entered a world in which we often cannot tell fact from fiction. Through greed and egocentric self-promotion, big tech organisations and their misguided recipients have a powerful tool in their hands: at best making the truth difficult to decipher, at worse making the world's information redundant.

Polarisation

One of the biggest challenges we all face when forming our view of the world is polarisation: the division of two, or multiple, sharply contrasting opinions and beliefs. Misinformation and disinformation fuel polarisation by feeding us information we view, absorb and share on social media channels. Social media channels use sophisticated algorithms that monitor what we see. These computer calculations then pro-actively show us more posts, stories, articles and videos of a similar nature, all serving to reinforce what we have already digested.

The business model behind these algorithms means they work hard to keep us scrolling; serving up what we like or 'might' like, or, more importantly, might buy. They are designed to create personalised bubbles of content, which can form an echo chamber of our own bias and beliefs. Unchallenged, this only serves to reinforce elements of our world view that may not be entirely healthy for us, or worse, not even true, creating false, misleading and damaging narratives.

Modern-day polarisation

- **Politics:** left versus right - capitalism versus socialism – freedom of movement versus border control

- **Ecological breakdown:** truth vs hoax

- **COVID-19:** natural cause versus lab-made; pro-vaccine versus anti-vaccine

- **Conflict:** East versus West; truth versus propaganda

- **Human Rights:** diversity; equality; LGBTQIA+; Trans Rights

All these examples of polarisation directly relate to humanity's big five existential threats.

- How are we meant to avoid ecological breakdown if many people don't believe it is really happening?

- How are we meant to guarantee the avoidance of nuclear war if we are so polarised around who to believe or trust?

- How are we meant to avoid future widespread diseases if we are so polarised about how they begin, our trust in qualified researchers and scientists, and the validity and effectiveness of vaccinations?

- How are we ever meant to fully eradicate racism, inequality and injustice if we are so polarised politically and societally?

Our existential threats will become more real if we cannot address and fix the polarisation of our society, which is fundamentally fuelled by mis and disinformation. If we are not able to come together and get to the truth about the things that matter, then we, as a species, will not be able to apply critical thinking, open our minds, challenge our current world view and seek the truth.

It is no longer our ability to influence that counts, it is our ability not to be influenced that will change the course of our future.

Now reflect on your world view and locus of control. Can you see opportunities to challenge your current thinking, reassess your beliefs and seek a deeper understanding to find truth? Can you spot your bias, reject flawed, unsubstantiated information and once again become a critical thinker?

Note down which beliefs you hold, which would be useful to re evaluate.

… continued.

"A lie gets halfway around the world before the truth has a chance to get its pants on."

Winston Churchil[39]

Next, we're going to look at balancing our scales. With all the information and understanding we've gathered, it's time to get to the point!

Chapter 9
Balancing the Scales
Maintaining our mental well-being.

As we have explored up to this point in the book, the key to longevity of well-being and psychological stability for all human beings is a balance of the pain-pleasure scales. This balance can help us endure suffering, pain and adversity, as well as seek out pleasure, fulfilment and reward.

If the scales tip too far in either direction, we lose our balance and struggle to maintain mental well-being.

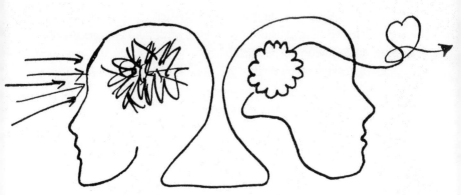

So let's quickly remind ourselves what happens if our scales tip too far one way or the other.

Too Much Pleasure

Before reading this book you may have thought, how on earth can it be a bad thing to experience too much pleasure? But, as we've discovered, if all we seek is comfort and pleasure, we alter our biochemistry in such a way that we become numb to its effects. Extreme levels of dopamine release on a continual basis, either chemically induced or adrenaline-fuelled, will ultimately alter our dopamine production, uptake and overall levels, leaving us regularly operating in a deficit.

The net result of a long-term dopamine deficit means we will struggle to feel the same high when engaging in dopamine-releasing events and experiences. Neuroscientists have also discovered that overexposure results in dopamine hits that don't last as long. So what used to be a pleasure-inducing experience, starts to habituate or attenuate – when something loses its interest, impact or force through over exposure or habit.

Think about an extreme dopamine release, either chemically induced (alcohol, drug use, tobacco) or adrenaline induced (extreme sports, gambling, sex). These can lead to addiction, as the only way to keep experiencing the highs of the pleasure response is to keep repeating and increasing the levels of activity. This explains why treatments are designed to tune down, reduce or eradicate the activity causing the addiction, helping to reset and normalise our dopamine response system. This, in turn, then allows us to feel the natural rewarding highs from periodic **Challenge** or **Neutral State** events again.

The pleasure system is not designed to be constant; it's designed to be intermittent and one of the greatest challenges for us and future generations is the expectation that we must have some form of pleasure and reward all the time.

We've established that for many rising and high-income economies, we live in a world of excess and consumption, of endless supply and immediacy of access. So you can start to see that when living a life of abundance, without exposure to challenge, hardship or pain, our scales start to tip towards the extreme side of pleasure. This, over time, leads to a weakened and more elusive pleasure response.

Regular exposure to high dopamine releasing activities results in lower baseline dopamine levels. Therefore a regular dopamine detox could help to keep the brain's pain-pleasure complex in balance. This is where the **Neutral State** can play an all important role.

Sometimes we simply have to be comfortable doing nothing!

Too Much Pain

We have also established that when we put ourselves into uncomfortable situations that involve challenge, uncertainty or pain, if temporary and aligned with a purpose or achievement-based endeavour, this can be an incredible contributor towards our motivation, performance and the reward we experience as a result. This represents the **Challenge State**. In this state we experience a relatively short, acute stress response to a situation that raises our motivation, attention and commitment to an endeavour, which carries risk or a level of importance to us. In this instance, dopamine can also be released, as the prospect of the reward comes to mind.

However, if we start to release too much adrenaline and cortisol on a long-term or extreme basis (even if we are achieving outcomes and goals) then, essentially, we will start to reduce the effects of the dopamine reward, whilst simultaneously impacting our physical and mental state. At this point we're entering a pattern of chronic stress. In a perverse way, chronic stress is interpreted as a 'badge of honour' for high-powered busy professionals, but at what cost to their performance and mental balance?

If you've ever experienced the feeling of burnout or becoming overwhelmed, these are strong indicators that you are experiencing chronic stress. Chronic or long-term levels of stress can lead to you being far more susceptible to perceiving situations as a Threat State, thus pushing your stress responses even higher to the detriment of your health and well-being.

To better understand this, think of stress as having three different stages: short, medium and long term. Let's explore them and their impact on us.

1. Short-term Stress

Generally, short-term stress can be good, even useful.

When an acute stress response is activated (fight or flight) to help us deal with a temporary and challenging situation, this would constitute short-term stress. For example, biologically this is designed to alert our immune system to fight infection, evolutionally it is designed to help us fight a threat that presents a true and immediate danger to our lives.

Think about our hunter-gatherers and their acute stress response to spotting a sabre-toothed tiger in the long grass. Well, our acute stress response, gifted to us by those ancient ancestors, remains the same and is achieved by priming our systems for better cognition, increased blood flow to the muscles, heightened levels of focus and a spike in our immune response. All designed to help us perform optimally in the face of challenge or danger.

Short-term stress is optimal for Threat and Challenge State situations often experienced by elite sports athletes during intense or pressurised competition, military personnel before and during operations, or a public speaker before delivering a keynote presentation in front of a large audience. The key to identifying short-term stress is that it's temporary, and after the situation or event has passed, the stress response deactivates, and you return to your Neutral State.

2. Medium-term Stress

A period of challenge, stress and duress that can prove both beneficial or difficult.

Troubling for some and useful for others, medium-term stress can play a role in increasing our overall stress threshold, as long as there is a breakpoint at the end of the stressful period.

Defined as lasting between a few days to a few weeks, medium-term stress is usually initiated by a single or series of triggers or circumstances within a short period of time. Our brains and bodies recognise that we are feeling stretched and strained and cannot find enough time to return to a Neutral State. Examples of this may be a heavy period of travel or intense workload; an ongoing and unresolved relationship challenge with a close friend or family member; financial constraints; or, maybe, a personal health issue. Whatever the trigger or circumstance, medium-term stress is perceived differently from person to person based on genetics, personality type, overall stress threshold and current mental state.

Some of us need periods of medium-term stress to grow and stretch ourselves; some will do all they can to avoid it, whilst others push into it reluctantly. What's important, however, is knowing that life will always present us with phases of medium-term stress and it's imperative that we can navigate and endure them. Not only does this increase our overall stress threshold, but it also strengthens the brain's neural pathways around tools, techniques and solutions for overcoming the challenges we're facing. If, therefore, we can limit and stagger the number of medium-term stress periods we encounter, then this will absolutely help us balance the pain-pleasure scales.

3. Long-term Stress

By and large long-term stress is debilitating and bad for us.

Categorised as consistent and ongoing for months or sometimes years on end, this unrelenting type of stress can be catastrophic for our mental and physical health, particularly for our heart and blood pressure. It also impacts other important areas of our general well-being, such as sleep, digestion and brain function.

Long-term stress puts us in a perpetual Threat State. This leads to increased levels of generalised anxiety and, if experienced over a long period of time, our ability to experience pleasure diminishes to near non-existent levels, along with our enjoyment of social connection, triumph or reward. In effect, we normalise low energy, low mood and anxiety, and suffer poor sleep – all symptomatic of low serotonin release and uptake in the brain, which can ultimately lead to a depressed state.

So, what causes long-term stress? Well, sometimes it's down to our natural biochemistry: an imbalance of brain chemicals that cause us to feel anxious, hypothetically worry or feel insignificant. Sometimes it's a by-product of an underlying ongoing health issue, or persistent, habitual and destructive patterns of thoughts, beliefs or behaviours, which repeatedly trigger the stress response. For example, an overly stressful or demanding job; a toxic relationship; an addiction or an unhealthy lifestyle.

Long-term stress can also be brought on by trauma, such as the loss of a loved one, being involved in an accident, a catastrophic event or a diagnosis of post-traumatic stress disorder (PTSD).

Given the highly detrimental impact long-term stress has on our mental and physical state, it is important to understand that when our scales tip into constant pain and distress, it can trigger a dangerous chain of events that will only serve to reduce our ability to receive pleasure, whilst normalising the feeling of pain. This is often where professional intervention and support is required.

So as we can see, too much pain or too much pleasure are equally suboptimal for us to be able to live a balanced and fulfilled life. Sometimes we may need professional or medical intervention to help us balance the scales. However, in general – and given our evolutionary programming, personality type, generational influences and view of the world – there is a hell of a lot most of us can do to help ourselves.

Let's start with Habituation.

Reducing Habituation
It's time to break the cycle

Habituation happens when we repeatedly focus on the same thing and it becomes less stimulating, even boring, resulting in the brain switching off as we lose interest.

Dr Tali Sharot is a leading professor of cognitive neuroscience and explores habituation in her book *Look Again: The Power of Noticing What was Already There*[40] co-authored with Cass R. Sunstein. In a discussion with the British Psychological Society in 2024, Sharot commented:

"When we become habituated to what brings us joy, the risk is that we quickly stop reacting to the happiness it can bring. Amazing food, great trips, expensive cars etc, will trigger a burst of joy if you experience them occasionally. But once those experiences become frequent, they stop producing real pleasure and instead they produce comfort, which is entirely different."

Dr Sharot is describing how, the more we habituate, the more we are likely to enter a "comfort crisis", as what we once found exhilarating, becomes no more than a Neutral State experience.

This explains why rock stars can become numb to the euphoria of performing in front of large audiences after months and months on a tour. Or why a mountain climber no longer experiences the same thrill and adrenaline rush after reaching their 100th summit.

But don't forget habituation is hard-wired into our evolution. Ultimately, we are built for routine and patterns of behaviour that support our number one core function of existence, survival. After all, a level of predictability gives us stability. But there is a difference between habituating in Neutral State activities, versus habituating in high dopamine-releasing activities and it's this, more concerning shift, that we see in society today.

Learning to dis-habituate

If we are to reset our brains when it comes to experiencing pleasure and reward, we need to break the cycle of habituation around things that are high dopamine releasing, especially activities with a high addictive liability, such as: social media, gambling, gaming, pornography, junk food or alcohol, even online shopping. But also, sometimes we just need to break our routines and switch our brains onto something new.

Two ways to break habituation (ideally you do both):

1.   Take a break from a repetitive activity.

2.   Introduce a new activity.

Think Intermittent Fasting!

An emerging area of research is forming around the concept of intermittent fasting[41]. This approach means you eat only within a defined time span in the day or week and its health benefits appear to include weight loss, the increase of our 'good' gut microbes and a decrease in cognitive decline.

Well, we need to apply the same concept to pain and pleasure.

Pleasure exists from incomplete desires.

It's our anticipation and the absence of something that creates the dopamine release and the motivation that follows. If we over habituate an experience, we run the risk of becoming numb to it and the brain switches off. If we, therefore, apply an intermittent approach to pleasure-inducing activities, instead of a continuous and habitual approach, then our brains will not switch off from their rewarding effects.

> Think about a song you love. If you hear it once a week you will crank up the volume and sing your heart out. If you hear it five times a day you will quickly get sick of it. Think about your relationship with your partner if you spend some healthy time apart throughout the week, you can't wait to see them when you get home, whereas, if you live 18 hours a day in each other's company, you can quickly start to get irritated by each other. If you wear the same aftershave or perfume every day of your life you stop smelling it, if you buy a brand new one, the smell seems to be vibrant and clear.

We are animals built for a degree of stability and routine; however, we also need a healthy balance of variation and challenge.

If you want to balance the pain-pleasure scales, you need to break your cycle of habituation, specifically around high dopamine-releasing activities with high addictive liability. This will enable your brain to refresh its interest and not switch off from the things that once gave you great pleasure and reward.

Managing Emotions

Get your butterflies flying in formation

Another key aspect of rebalancing our pain and pleasure scales is our ability to interpret and manage our emotions, thoughts and feelings better and more effectively.

Emotions serve an important purpose. A direct result of chemical responses in the brain from cortisol, dopamine, oxytocin, serotonin and adrenaline, our emotions exist primarily to help us fulfil our three core functions of human existence – survival, reproduction and purpose. Without them we would not be the dominant species we are today. But, if we are going to get better at dealing with Challenge and Threat State situations, we must get better at enduring pain and discomfort. Which means we must get better at recognising, interpreting and managing our emotions. Most importantly the emotion of fear.

Fear taps into our overarching core function of survival and because of this it's our most powerful emotion. Fear can spur us on or overwhelm us; we can leap into action or be frozen on the spot.

I often explain to people that **fear is twice as crippling as desire will ever be motivating**, yet fear is normal and necessary; it's always going to be part of our lives, so we must learn to manage it. The best way to do that is to better understand it, and bring what is usually unconscious responses into our conscious mind.

Achieving Emotional Granularity

Categorising emotions in the moment

Emotional granularity is an individual's ability to recognise, differentiate and identify emotions with precision and specificity. Neuroscientist and psychologist Lisa Feldman Barrett discusses this in her book *How Emotions are Made: The Secret Life of the Brain*[42], Feldman Barrett states that, *"Emotional granularity is your ability to understand and differentiate specific emotions. People with high emotional granularity are able to better cope with stress and* *negative emotions... It means rather than just identifying that you feel 'bad', you're able to construct and identify a variety of more specific emotional concepts such as: angry, grumpy, aggravated, annoyed, worried, scared, gloomy or sad."*

Emotional granularity is important, because if you can identify what type of emotion you are feeling in the moment, then you have a better chance of identifying the trigger that caused it, which then gives you the ability to deal with it.

Here at T2 we do a lot of work with individuals on managing personal triggers, which is fundamentally aimed at helping them build greater levels of emotional granularity. The more information you establish in times of pain and discomfort, the better equipped you will be to deal with it.

If you break pain and discomfort down to a simple formula then you can conclude that there are two types: **physical** and **mental**. Within these two types there are three circumstances in which they can occur: in the **past**, the **present** or the **future**.

Physical Past	**Physical Present**	**Physical Future**
Something that caused me physical pain or discomfort in the past.	Something that is causing me physical pain or discomfort right now.	Something that I perceive may cause me physical pain and discomfort in the future.
Previous accident	A tough workout	Becoming ill
Serious Injury	Headache	Accident
Abusive relationship	Chronic pain	Dying

Physical pain and discomfort can cause us to go into Threat State and unless we can pinpoint which type (Past, Present or Future) is causing our emotional response, then it will prove difficult to deal with.

Mental Past	Mental Present	Mental Future
Something that caused me mental pain or discomfort in the past.	Something that is causing me mental pain or discomfort right now.	Something that I perceive may cause me mental pain and discomfort in the future.
Negative feedback	Speaking in public	Fear of losing a loved one
Losing a job	Argument with a friend	Financial worries
Relationship breakup	Stressful experience	Fear of Failure

Mental pain and discomfort can cause us to go into Threat State and unless we can pinpoint which type (Past, Present or Future) is causing our emotional response, then it will prove difficult to deal with.

To identify your emotional triggers, ask yourself two questions…

1. Is my pain and discomfort relating to physical or mental circumstances?

2. Are these circumstances in the past, the present or the future?

If you can develop the ability to ask yourself these simple questions when feeling compromised, stressed or emotionally elevated, then you are consciously intervening and increasing the information available from which you can try to respond accordingly, and not just simply react. This is **emotional granularity**.

If you form a habit of practising this, over time you will start to recognise patterns to your emotional responses. For example, I hardly ever have any Physical Past, Present or Future triggers and very few Mental Past, as I tend not dwell on the past and find it easy to move forward. However, nearly all my emotional triggers are either Mental Present or Mental Future, these seem to test me the most. From monitoring and getting specific about my own emotional responses I've concluded on the following:

- In the present I fear looking bad in front of others or being overly challenged or oppressed.

- In the future I fear failure or a lack of progress towards my goals. I also fear the prospect of not being financially sound.

With this personal insight in mind, I know that my emotions will spike, and I could struggle to endure pain and discomfort when I am…

Trigger	Feeling
Being kept from doing what I want to do.	I feel annoyed
Being told I'm wrong about something.	I feel annoyed
Being attacked or criticised.	I feel annoyed
Making slow progress towards my goals.	I feel frustrated
Failing in something I am responsible for.	I feel scared
Encountering slow-moving people or inaction.	I feel frustrated
Feeling undermined or made to look bad.	I feel annoyed
Feeling a lack of control or influence.	I feel anxious
Feeling a lack of ownership or accountability from others.	I feel frustrated

As you can see, I've managed to associate specific feelings with each trigger. Therefore, with two quick questions and a bit of reflection, I'm able to identify a trigger and its associated emotion. I can then get on with ABC'ing the hell out of it!

Remember: Acknowledge – Breathe – Control?

Acknowledge – what is triggering you.

Breath – for 90 seconds to reduce the effects of cortisol.

Control – focus on the things you control, make decisions and take action.

Now, it's worth mentioning – and my wife would agree – that I am far from perfect with this approach, after all, I'm human and I am trying to intercept and interpret powerful emotions that have evolved over hundreds of thousands of years. But just by following this process I am building greater levels of emotional granularity all the time. Try it. After a while you will become very aware, very quickly about what triggers you and why. Your brain will then start to recognise patterns to these triggers and can even start predicting them.

Maybe take a moment now to think about and capture which circumstances are the main cause of your emotional triggers; Physical or Mental; Past, Present or Future? For the circumstances you identify, how does it make you feel? When you know this you can start thinking about some coping mechanisms to better deal with emotions when they arise.

Trigger	Feeling

It's worth noting here the complex interplay between mental and physical pain and discomfort, whether past, present or future. For example, some people we work with share that they are extremely anxious about future physical pain and discomfort, in fact their greatest fear is becoming ill or dying. However, they reveal that the origins of this is due to a past trauma. So the interplay is that it's a Mental Past trigger leading to a repetitive Physical Future trigger. And this interplay can come in many forms and complex variations.

If you want to balance the pain-pleasure scales you must get better at enduring pain and discomfort. One of the keys to achieving this lies in the ability to manage your emotions. So, let's get your butterflies flying in formation... Work on developing emotional granularity, allowing you to recognise, differentiate and identify emotions with precision and specificity. To achieve this, use my simple formula for identifying and categorising your personal triggers. Then, with a healthy dose of courage and durability, you can Acknowledge, Breathe and Control your way through life, enduring the pain and discomfort you encounter in a healthier, more robust and resilient way.

The High Road, Low Road Balance

It's time to get used to being uncomfortably comfortable!

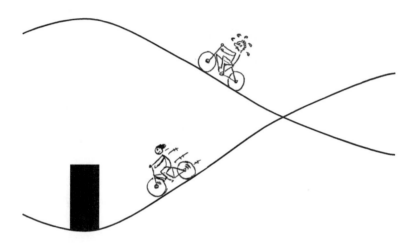

Earlier on in the book I talked about the High Road, Low Road motivation dilemma. When it comes to our motivation to do something, our brain quickly and subconsciously assesses the situation, applying a sequencing called Duration – Path – Outcome. Simply put, the brain is asking:

- How long is this going to take me?
- What effort is required from me?
- What's the outcome at the end?

The result of this lightning-fast process is the decision our brain will come to on whether this is a Low Road or High Road situation. To recap:

The Low Road describes a situation or activity that gives immediate or timely relief, results, gains or gratification; you will get a quick reward and the effort and commitment is likely to be minimal or easily achievable.

The High Road describes a situation or activity that offers delayed relief, results, gains or gratification; you will not necessarily see quick rewards and it's likely to involve personal sacrifice, effort and commitment over a longer period to achieve the goal. It may also carry some risk.

During early evolutionary periods, our brains would assess requirements prioritising survival, reproduction and purpose, and decide whether we're looking at a High Road or Low Road situation. To preserve energy and effort the brain would try to prioritise Low Road situations and activities. We therefore became more attracted to and comfortable being motivated by the Low Road. After all, why wouldn't we prioritise something that delivers results for less effort, whilst preserving energy that we may require later?

The challenge for hunter-gatherers was the lack of Low Road situations in their environment. Maybe foraging for plants and shrubs or picking low-hanging fruit may have constituted the Low Road, assuming they easily found a flourishing patch of fruit trees. However, to survive they had to push into the High Road on a regular basis.

Fast forward to today, and as we have established, we live in a world where for most of us, in almost every situation we face, there is a Low Road motivation alternative. Our brains still perform the Duration – Path – Outcome sequence to assess where we should expend our energy and effort. But, without doubt, there are far more Low Road alternatives than there were for our ancestors. This combination of brain sequencing and a world with an abundance of comfort is resulting in us becoming Low Road motivation machines – a situation which requires us to switch off our autopilot and take back control.

Choosing the High Road over the Low Road

The Elevator

You return to the office after your lunch break. You need to get back to the 9th floor where your desk is based. Your brain performs a quick Duration – Path – Outcome sequence and in a nanosecond you have your options.

Option 1: High Road – Take the stairs, there are ten flights (approx. 100 stairs), it will take you five minutes and you will have to expend some energy and effort to get there. It will hurt a little on the legs and you will arrive out of breath. However, this will provide health benefits if you form a habit of this over time.

Option 2: Low Road – Take the lift, press nine, you will be at your floor in 60 seconds. Little energy or effort is required but zero health benefit.

Research in the US suggests that only 2% of Americans take the stairs over the option of the elevator. Despite the clear physical benefits of the stairs[43] we are highly programmed to take the Low Road option. Gaining widespread use by the early 20th century[44], once popularly accepted, elevators hailed the beginning of the change to our modern-day sedentary urban lifestyles.

If you want to balance the High and Low Road, take the stairs...

The Takeaway

You leave work and after a long day, your attention turns to what you are going to have for evening dinner. Your brain performs a quick Duration – Path – Outcome sequence and in a nanosecond you have options.

Option 1: High Road – Stop off at the supermarket, pick up some fresh ingredients, and once home, make a healthy meal full of fresh, wholesome produce. It will cost you an extra 45 minutes on your commute home, then an additional 45 minutes to prepare and cook your meal, plus the clean-up operation afterwards. There are clear nutritional and health benefits of cooking from scratch with fresh, wholesome ingredients.

Option 2: Low Road – Go straight home and order a takeaway. In fact, if you order it now on your phone app it's just three clicks and by the time you get home, you'll probably meet the delivery driver outside your door. No time or energy required and tasty food. However, the high fat, salt and sugar content is likely to be detrimental to your nutritional and overall health.

According to a 2022 UK survey of 2,000 people, 49% reported eating takeaway food up to four times a week[45]. Our eating habits have significantly changed over the course of the last ten years. COVID-19 and the emergence of instant ordering via phone apps has meant that the Low Road alternative to home-prepared meals is much more accessible.

If you want to balance the High and Low Road, go shopping and make the meal...

The Gym

After several weeks of no exercise, you decide to get back into the gym. You decide you will start on Monday. Monday arrives. By the end of the day you're feeling tired with zero motivation. Your brain performs a quick Duration – Path – Outcome sequence and in a nanosecond you have options.

Option 1: High Road – Go home, don't sit down, get your gym clothes and trainers together and go to the gym. It's going to be painful, sweaty and you're going to hurt. It will likely take up two hours of your evening and, to reap the full benefits, you're going to have to have a self-prepared healthy meal when you get home later. Oh, and tomorrow you're going to ache like crazy. To top it off, you won't notice any difference for your efforts immediately. Yet, the health benefits in the long run are vast and the fact you've made a start is a huge psychological boost.

Option 2: Low Road – Go home, and ease your way back into activity with a casual ten-minute dog walk. Don't stretch yourself too soon. This way you can have dinner earlier because you're absolutely starving, right? A short walk is better than nothing and you will definitely go to the gym tomorrow, won't you?!

Research done by Fridge Raiders in 2019 reported that, amongst the UK population, £4 billion per year was wasted on unused UK gym memberships. Today, with the uplift in gym membership fees, this amount is likely to be over £5.6 billion[46]. The desire to take the High Road and work out three or four times a week is certainly there; however, it's the temptation of the Low Road alternatives that sabotage our plans for better health time and time again.

If you want to balance the High and Low Road, go to the gym, sports club, dance class, or whatever it is that gives you a workout.

The Night Out

Your close friends have arranged a much-needed night out. You haven't seen a lot of each other over recent years due to the demands of work and family life. The day arrives and after a busy day you're feeling tired and starting to question if you can be bothered. Your brain performs a quick Duration – Path – Outcome sequence and in a nanosecond you have options.

Option 1: High Road – Go home, get a shower, listen to some music, book the taxi and go and enjoy an evening with your friends. It's going to take some energy and effort, but the rewards of catching up with friends and socialising will be good for you and your mental health. If nothing else it's a chance to switch off from the chaos of life, work and kids for just a few hours and have fun with friends.

Option 2: Low Road – Message your friends with an excuse that you don't feel well, after all you really can't be bothered. Go home, get into your pyjamas and lie on the sofa all night watching TV. Little effort for an easy night, right? Until later when you see photos of your friends having fun on social media and you start to regret your decision. You're now feeling isolated, regretful and are experiencing serious FOMO.

It's long been recognised that being social supports our mental health. In 2016, in an article published in *Psychology Today*, Angela K. Troyer Ph.D., C. Psych. explored how socialising with friends and close connections provides several benefits to physical and mental health[47], including:

- Increasing overall mental well-being
- Boosting the immune system
- Reducing risk of dementia

If you want to balance the High and Low Road, make time for friends.

The Job

You have been in your current job for three years. It's a secure role and it pays quite well but you are unfulfilled and bored. You're now finding going to work a chore and you don't have a great relationship with your manager, or an incentive to fix the situation. Your brain performs a quick Duration – Path – Outcome sequence and in a nanosecond you have options.

Option 1: High Road – You believe you can do whatever you set your mind to. Time to update your CV, start networking and making enquiries about roles you feel would ignite your interest and passion; it might even mean retraining. Yes, it may mean some uncomfortable interviews, along with some potential setbacks and rejection. There's the financial uncertainty of losing a good pay packet and possible unemployment, but what's the price of happiness and fulfilment? You're proud of your skills and they're being wasted so come on, let's go for it!

Option 2: Low Road – You're on to a good thing; yes, the job is dull, but it's secure and the pay is good. It's not exactly making you unhappy to the point of depression and there's too much risk in leaving, after all you have bills to pay. You can put up with the manager, hopefully they'll move on soon. So keep your head down, don't stress yourself, you're lucky to have a job after all...

The job site Indeed's 2022 UK *Workplace Happiness Survey*[48] reported that 21% of respondents don't feel happy at work most of the time, with 19% not feeling energised in most of their tasks. Feeling unhappy is second only to poor pay when it comes to people considering leaving their role with over 90% reporting that their mood at home is affected by their happiness (or lack of it) at work.

The average person is likely to spend 90,000 hours at work during their lifetime. That's approximately one third of their life.

A similar survey in 2021 reported that 95% of respondents believed happiness at work is possible, so don't settle.

If you want to balance the High and Low Road, find a job that you like and you're good at, that finances a lifestyle you're happy with.

We've explored just five examples of the High versus Low Road in action. Remember, however, taking the Low Road can often be beneficial and the right thing to do, especially if you need some rest and recuperation in **Neutral State**. But you must guard against habituation when it comes to a pattern of continuous Low Road choices. You must push yourself to find a good balance by taking the High Road in situations and circumstances where the benefits may take more effort and pain, but the results will be significantly better for your mental and physical health, and that of those around you.

Enemy of the States

Embrace neutral, deal with the threat and rise to the challenge.

In this final section on balancing the scales, let's now revisit the three psychological states of the pain-pleasure complex and interrogate why it is so important for us to find the balance. We need to make peace with all our 'states' and not see them as the enemy.

Here's a quick recap before a deeper dive with tools to help us navigate each state successfully.

 1. Neutral State: in this state we avoid pain, seek comfort and our motivation is towards pleasure and contentment. It is our comfort zone. At home with our feet up watching a movie, pottering in the garden, snoozing on the sofa or taking a gentle walk. Neither stressed nor elated. We are at 'rest' and experiencing recovery.

 2. Challenge State: in this state we seek pleasure and reward, yet to do so will involve us enduring some pain. Our motivation is towards pleasure through reward and fulfilment. We are out of our comfort zone, we may be taking on a complex role at work, moving house or even writing a book. We're experiencing stress, risk and feeling challenged, but all in a bid to achieve a goal or reward.

 3. Threat State: in this state we seek to avoid an immediate or perceived threat and our motivation is purely to survive. We may be operating at a height, public speaking, confronted by an aggressor, plunging into deep water or taking on board unexpected news from the doctor, all of which can put us into Threat State.

1. The Neutral State

Busy doing nothing…

From the thousands of data points and studies we have gathered here at T2 around personality types, motivations and world views, we know first-hand that some people are very comfortable doing nothing, whilst others find that it makes them anxious. Some people thrive in the comfort of routine, safety, predictability and low chaos and, therefore, more often than not, they seek the Neutral State. Others can become irritated, bored and frustrated if they spend too much time in their Neutral State and like to embrace a little more challenge and chaos in their life.

Either way, the Neutral State is important for ALL humans. The amount of time each person requires in this state will differ depending on their wiring, but without question we all need it, we all need to rest, recuperate and recharge in order to return to our baseline state. Being busy can feel like a badge of honour, but this is foolish, and there are plenty of good reasons why we should give our brains a break.

Information and Focus

When we are in Neutral State, our brain retracts from focusing on a single problem or situation; it stops taking in large amounts of information and the need to process it at speed. Our whole system slows down and our senses and focus become broader and clearer. Imagine riding a bike at full speed for five miles. You're going to be pretty tired by the end and all your focus will have been on peddling, steering and on your direct line of sight. Now, imagine cruising through the countryside at a relaxed and leisurely speed for five miles. At the end you won't have expended a great deal of energy, and you will have seen, smelt and heard an array of things along the way, which has led to a much more conscious and rich experience.

Finding time for Neutral State is restorative for our energy and our mood. It provides us with the opportunity to slow down our information consumption and widen our focus.

Attention
When in Neutral State, the brain operates predominantly in the default mode network (DMN). The DMN plays an important role in our ability to focus inward, rather than on the external world. The DMN helps us with reflection, memories, ideas and creativity; it also allows us to sit and consider closely how we are feeling and connect with our self-worth.

Basically in the absence of any Challenge or Threat, the Neutral State enables us to completely shift our attention to our internal thoughts, as we are not required to perform high-speed, complex processing of our external world. Our DMN is incredibly important and restorative, as long as it's for an optimal amount of time because, those who spend too much time in Neutral State and, therefore, have an excessive amount of time to internally focus, can suffer counterproductive effects. Reflection can turn into procrastination; memories can provoke anxiety; self-worth can turn into self-loathing. You can see why the key to our mental well-being is the ability to switch between our states and not spend excessive amounts of time in any one of them.

Problem Solving
Humans are good at problem solving, after all its brought us this far, and we can apply problem solving in any of the three psychological states. However, the most optimal state for problem solving is our Neutral State. One of the main reasons for this is our emotions (or lack of them).

When we are in Neutral State, we are not experiencing the extreme levels or effects of either positive or negative emotions. We are on an even keel, in control and relatively calm. When an issue arises, this allows us to combine any emotional response with rational thought and do a couple of things really well:

1. Reduce bias and dissonance – we're less likely to have a reactive, preset position.

2. Enhance critical thinking – we're more likely to look at the problem objectively, seeking facts from which to draw reasonable conclusions.

The Neutral State plays an important role in our lives. However, if you are reading this and spend most of you time in yours, then it's likely not serving you too well, whether that's procrastination, lack of self-worth and purpose, increased anxiety, hypothetical worrying or just plain boredom. Letting the mind have time to reflect and wander is important, but in small doses and at the right time. Allowing it to do so for days, weeks or months will, without doubt, start to tip your scales out of balance.

Likewise, if you are reading this and you are spending hardly any time in your Neutral State, you will also be feeling the effects. This may be in the form of burnout, fatigue, high stress, irritability or disorganisation. Remember, if you never enter a state of rest and recuperation your brain's system is going to be operating on full gas all the time, processing copious amount of information whilst being completely focused on your external world, never taking time to look internally, reflect and relax.

Tips for making time for our Neutral State:

- **Prioritise It** – decide on the trade-offs, what are you saying no to?

- **Schedule It** – put it in your diary and protect it at all costs!

- **Remove It** – time out from technological devices, social media, stressful travel and stressful people.

We have not evolved over millions of years to remain in one state for too long. But you must find time for your Neutral State, and you must become comfortable in it. You also need to find the courage to push out of it when it's time to shift focus and energy and seek something more stimulating, challenging and rewarding. That's where we are heading next.

2. The Challenge State

Lets go, we can do this...

Just as the Neutral State plays a vital role in supporting rest, recuperation, reflection and internal thinking, the Challenge State is crucial for building resilience, competence and confidence.

Some of us relish being in a Challenge State situation while some of us feel like it's a little too far outside our comfort zone. Some of us may even catastrophise a challenge and quickly head into Threat State instead. If that's something you find yourself doing, don't worry – we're coming to that shortly. Whatever you relate to, just remember this: the Challenge State plays a very important role in our ability to exist, function, grow and succeed in the chaos and complexity of modern-day life.

There are so many situations and instances in life which require us to be in a Challenge State. If you think about it, anything that does not present a true and immediate danger to our lives, but carries a level of uncertainty, risk or difficulty, constitutes a challenge. This could be as simple as driving on the motorway, delivering a presentation, navigating the London Tube network, playing sports, going for a job interview or having an uncomfortable conversation. It could also represent something big and life changing, such as starting a business, moving house, getting married, completing a degree or climbing Mount Everest.

Ultimately, we are trying to achieve something tangible that will come with a reward, but also comes with risk, uncertainly and potential consequence. Our brains, however, don't possess the ability to accurately separate and control the stress response accordingly. As we have explored, what was once designed to trigger our fight or flight response in the face of immediate danger is now trying to decipher between what really is immediate danger versus what is making us feel uncomfortable, exposed or afraid. For example, we can safely say that giving a public presentation is not going to kill you, but the level of adrenaline, anxiety and fear some people feel around the activity can reach the similar levels to that of swimming with sharks. I know this because I have seen it myself and have coached many senior executives who are terrified of public speaking. So our brains have this discrepancy in their ability to accurately produce the optimal stress response based on the severity of the actual risk. Combine this with the fact that we are all wired and programmed in our unique way and how we cope with situations differs, you can start to see why some people are very capable in Challenge State and others not so.

We can all agree, however, that we must push ourselves into a Challenge State if we want to get on in life. To quote American psychologist and best-selling author Susan Jeffers, we must *Feel the Fear and Do It Anyway*[49]. Otherwise, we will be stuck on a never ending seesaw between Neutral and Threat states. This is not a good position to be in because, in the absence of being able to correctly interpret stressors and situations as a challenge, we are only ever going to be comfortable or catastrophising.

Tips for rising to the challenge:

1. **Plan and organise** – if you know you're going to do or be responsible for something, think about it beforehand. Plan and be organised, as this will help you identify potential issues and be calmer in the face of unforeseen circumstances.

2. **ABC the hell out of it** – Acknowledge – Breathe – Control, take control of a situation by using this simple three-step technique and stop the sensations of anxiety in their tracks. Check back to page 78 to remind yourself of this technique.

3. **Challenge Staging, Challenge Observing and Challenge Statistics**, breakdown a challenge into smaller achievable goals; find and learn from others taking on a similar challenges; find evidence to help you rationalise your fears. Check back to page 91 to remind yourself of this technique.

4. **Eyes on the Prize** – visualise your path to your reward and, through doing so, gain confidence and keep motivated to reach your goal. Bring it alive in your mind. Check back to page 87 to remind yourself of this technique.

5. **Open Gaze** – lift your head up to widen your window of focus. What resources are available to you to help address a problem? Who has the skills to complement your own? Check back to page 99 to remind yourself of this technique.

We can learn and practise the ability to correctly identify our stress response, interpret our emotions through **emotional granularity**, and push ourselves into situations which, yes, will stretch us, but will also help us to grow in competence and confidence. However, in the aftermath of a Challenge State situation fuelled by dopamine, cortisol and adrenaline, we will probably need to retract for some much needed Neutral State time in order to reset and recharge.

This explains why after returning from a long holiday involving stressful travel, you need a sofa day, or why after a busy and challenging week at work you're ready to curl up in bed at 9pm. But in both these cases you do so feeling happy, satisfied and fulfilled because you have experienced or achieved something worthwhile. This post-Challenge State elation is something we cannot derive from the Neutral State or, even worse, from the dreaded Threat State.

If you are reading this though, and you are pushing too hard, too often into continuous Challenge State situations, then start to think where you can find that much-needed time to retract to the Neutral State.

If you are reading this and, by your own acknowledgement, you are not pushing into Challenge State enough, then look for the opportunities to do so, because this will go a long way towards you being able to strengthen your resolve, build your confidence, find meaning and ultimately balance your pain-pleasure scales.

The more you push into Challenge State, the more mental courage, durability and resilience you will build and – guess what? You're going to need this in abundance from time to time when your brain inevitably pushes you into a Threat State...

3. The Threat State

The panic of impending doom…

The third and final psychological state we can be in at any one time is the dreaded Threat State. The state of panic or feeling of impending doom designed to keep us alive has served us well throughout our evolution, and if you think back to the most scared or frightened you have ever been in your life, then you will be able to resonate with what it feels like to be in true or immediate danger. But very few things in modern-day life present a true or immediate danger to your life. Some of us have been unlucky enough to have experienced it in the form of accidents, serious illnesses, tragedies and atrocities but, in the main, most of us haven't.

As we have explored, the number of people experiencing anxiety and depression are on the rise; the modern-day "comfort crisis" is throwing our pain and pleasure balance out of kilter aided by the impact of generational shift and the digital industrial revolution. We are experiencing greater levels of perceived panic and impending doom than ever before. The good news, thankfully, is that in most situations this response is driven by perception and not necessarily reality. These perceptions are heavily influenced by the sheer amount of information we can access or are exposed too. And remember what we explored in the previous chapter: a large proportion of this information is actually misinformation or disinformation.

You find a lump on your skin and two Google searches later you've self-diagnosed skin cancer…

You click on your social media feed and there's breaking news of climate change, conflict, shootings, disease, recession and corruption…

You're happily watching videos of cats playing on your phone, yet within three clicks you stumble across something violent or pornographic…

Your smart watch tells you for the 57th day in a row that your BMI is high, resting heart rate is suboptimal and you're not getting enough steps in…

Your WhatsApp is pinging like crazy with conflict and drama kicking going off in your friends' group…

Scientists have discovered that almost every product in your bathroom cabinet may cause cancer…

Your energy provider messages you to say your gas and electric bill is increasing for the third quarter in a row…

Sugar is bad for you…

Meat is bad for you…

Carbs are bad for you…

Fat is bad for you…

Gluten is bad for you…

Dairy is bad for you….

Illegal immigration is overwhelming our social services…

The NHS is doomed and people are dying in corridors…

Smoking kills, vaping is the healthier alternative … then the Government bans disposable vapes over emerging health concerns…

A meteor the size of New York has is heading straight for Earth…

Caffeine is bad for you…

Too much fruit is bad for you…

We are on the cusp of World War III…

These messages could easily represent one day's information input into your brain. ONE DAY! Tomorrow the cycle will be repeated, and the next, and the next.

On top of this information overload there are other everyday situations which can put us in a Threat State.

Someone moves in on our territory at work or fires a finger-pointing email to us and copies in our boss. Maybe you're on a performance plan and there a real risk you could lose your job. Maybe it's personal issues that are putting you in a Threat State, such as financial worries, health challenges, parental responsibilities and so on.

Now again, none of these present a true or immediate danger to your life, but it doesn't stop your brain producing a similar fight or flight response and it certainly doesn't stop you from feeling completely exposed, threatened or fearful. But those who can navigate a Threat State situation, whether real or perceived, are able to follow an effective three-step mental process to regulate their response and act with self-knowledge.

Let's use the above example of the shitty email: we read the first few lines of the email and our brain kicks in and says, *"Here we go!"*, we feel a rising panic, our stomach tightens, our mouths suddenly dry, we feel too warm… Step 1 requires us to take a moment and ask ourselves some important questions.

Step 1. Identify – what is causing me to feel threatened?

Considering the emotional and chemical response associated with a Threat State, the first step is to pause, take a moment (which is why the ABC technique works so well) and try to establish and identify the root cause of what's causing the Threat State. Try to work back to the most granular level possible.

i) What's the Trigger?

It's that email that came in from my colleague out of the blue this morning with my boss copied in. It has made me feel angry and exposed, I'm worrying that my credibility is compromised and ultimately, I might lose my job.

ii) Why did my colleague send that email?

Because they're a dick? No, seriously, because their project is at risk of overrunning so maybe they're panicking too. Maybe they're in Threat State themselves.

iii) Ok, so why is this situation putting them in a Threat State?

Probably because they have similar fears to me around credibility and job security, after all they must fear the kick back from the boss too.

By asking yourself a few questions and getting as granular as you can, you can really start to identify what's causing you to feel threatened and what the root cause behind it is. This will settle your body's system and you can calmly move on to Step 2.

Step 2. Assess — is this a perceived or real threat?

Now assess whether the threat you are experiencing is real or perceived. Again asking the right questions is key.

i) Has this email exposed me?

Potentially, or maybe it presents an opportunity to show how I can be supportive and helpful.

ii) Is my credibility compromised?

Thinking about it, not really.

iii) Am I likely to lose my job?

Highly unlikely.

The result of this stage means you have established that the initial Threat State feeling is perceived and not real and therefore a catastrophic outcome is unlikely.

Step 3. Manage – what do I need to do to either deal with, or re-frame the threat?

Ok, so we are now well on our way to navigating our way out of this Threat State and hopefully we are a few steps away from returning to a Challenge, or even Neutral State. We have identified the root cause of the threat and established that it's more perceived than real, so now we need to move forward and act.

i) How do I need to respond to this situation?
Respond by email, acknowledge the situation and offer immediate support to my colleague. Suggest a meeting as soon as possible.

ii) Do I cc my boss?
Yes, just so everyone is in the loop, making it clear that I am cooperating with my colleague about finding a solution.

iii) Do I mention to my colleague how the email out the blue made me feel?
Yes, honesty is the best policy, they need to know how I felt when I received it. Doing this face-to-face will be best and hopefully we can agree a better way to manage issues in the future.

This is clearly a workplace example and there will be lots of instances in your personal life that will put you in a Threat State. The same process applies:

- Identify what is causing the threat.

- Assess if the threat is real or perceived.

- Manage the situation with decision and actions.

Becoming accomplished at recognising your states (Neutral, Challenge or Threat), what they look like, feel like, how you act, behave and communicate when in each of them, means you will start to build greater levels of emotional granularity. This ability alone gives you a degree of control because, as part of the process, you are simultaneously building greater levels of situational awareness and will be able to make decisions and take actions accordingly. After all,

"There is nothing more powerful than the made-up mind."

Lewis Pugh[50]

The key to mental well-being is to balance our psychological scales.

All three mental states serve a purpose in our lives. All three are as important as each other. All three, if working in collaboration, operate like a well-oiled machine. However, we are not built to spend too much time in any one of them. If one of them slows down, speeds up or stops working, our machine, our brain, will struggle to perform optimally. This is why balancing our pain-pleasure scales is so important.

So what does the future hold? Can we get back to the essentials of what it means to be human? Will being human fundamentally change? Let's finish our journey by looking at what might be in store for us all in the coming years.

Chapter 10

The Future

Preparing for better mental health.

In February 2024, funded by the Health Foundation[51], the Resolution Foundation[52] published a report on young people's health in the UK. *We've only just begun: Action to improve young people's mental health, education and employment* by Charlie McCurdy and Louise Murphy[53] follows a three-year research programme exploring young people's relationship between mental health and employment.

McCurdy and Murphy explored a range of issues, including how insecure work impacts mental health, the prevalence of low hours for young people entering employment and the crossover of mental health, employment and geography.

Here are some findings from the report:

- Over one-in-three (34%) of young people aged 18–24 reported symptoms that indicated they were experiencing a common mental health disorder (CMD), such as: depression, anxiety or bi-polar. This is a big increase since 2000 when one-in-four (24%) reported these symptoms.

- Young people with mental health problems are more likely to be out of work than their healthy peers. Between 2018 and 2022, one in five (21%) of 18–24-year-olds with mental health problems were workless, compared to 13% of those without mental health problems.

- Universities have become hotbeds for mental health problems: the share of young full-time students with a CMD has increased at a far faster rate than that of working or out-of-work young people.

- A shocking four-in-five (79%) of 18–24-year-olds who are workless due to ill health only have qualifications at GCSE-level or below, compared to one-third (34%) of all people in that age group.

- Mental health problems are blighting young people's education. An estimated one-in-eight (12%) of 11–16-year-olds with poor mental health problems missed more than 15 days of school in the autumn term of 2023 compared to just 2% of their healthier classmates.

The report also points out that, because of the rise of mental health disorders, more than half a million 18–24-year-olds in the UK were prescribed anti-depressants in 2021–22.

Considering that the subjects of this report consist largely of Generation Z and Generation Alpha, two generations that will form the major contributors to our society over the next 50 years, it is incredibly important that we focus all our efforts to both support and enable this group to develop better mental and physical health. As we have explored throughout this book, these young people's ability to balance their pain and pleasure scales will be a crucial element in this process.

Now, it goes without saying that no one can accurately predict the future, but we can look at trends and draw upon experiences throughout evolution and human history to predict some likely future patterns.

From what I experience, observe and learn from the thousands of people we engage with at T2 annually, I believe the answer to balancing our future pain-pleasure scales lies in influencing three key areas: **parental, societal** and **educational**.

Parental Influence – building mental fortitude through the balance of boundaries and self-expression.

The parental influence of Generation X, Millennials and early Generation Z over the next 30 years is going to play a crucial role in addressing and stemming the rising tide of poor mental health.

As we explored in Chapter 7, continual generational shift has seen a change in parental guidance and philosophy. From the stoic, highly disciplined approach of the Silent Generation, when young people were to be seen and not heard, to the much more liberal modern-day approach where a young person's voice, their needs and wants, is paramount. Extreme examples perhaps, but the truth is that neither of these parenting approaches is optimal.

In this book, I have presented a large amount of psychological and science-based evidence pointing to the fact that human psychological stability, resilience and fulfilment lies in our ability to balance our pain and pleasure scales effectively. This enables us to switch between, and be able to cope with, our three psychological states. I would therefore suggest that parenting needs to be focused around giving children the skills and knowledge required to endure pain and discomfort, whilst seeking out and experiencing pleasure and reward, placing as much focus on enduring pain, as on seeking pleasure and comfort. To achieve this, we need to re-embrace parental concepts, such as discipline, boundaries, consequence and scarcity, whilst remaining progressive with encouragement, reinforcement and self-expression.

It is OK to set boundaries and expectations for children. It helps them to develop the ability to operate within a structure or set of guidelines and rules. This equips them well for life and work.

It is OK to discipline children if they cross these boundaries, as it helps them to understand that there are consequences to dysfunctional or damaging behaviour.

It is OK to say no to children, even if you possess the ability to say yes. It helps them learn to be patient and become resourceful. It also helps them to appreciate the small things; things you can't buy but which bring joy and happiness.

Just as balance is the key to mental well-being and fortitude, it is also the key to good parenting.

Throughout my research, work and experience I believe parenting is the most influential and impactful factor on the formation of our children's personality style and world view. That may sound daunting for parents and care givers to read, but it's true. We are not going to get it right all the time, but if we try to strike the right balance it means we will get it right more often than not.

The brain doesn't fully form in its structural and mechanical capacity until the early 20s, so our children are heavily dependent on parents and primary care givers to guide, advise and direct throughout childhood and adolescence. This is why extreme philosophies of authoritative or highly liberal parenting tend to fall short. But it doesn't have to be at either end of the scale! Learning when to be more authoritative versus when we can be more empowering and trusting is the key to balanced parenting.

Before all else, we must offer unconditional love, care and affection to our children, yet not be afraid to have boundaries and discipline without volatility or rage.

Societal Influence – thriving and surviving in a fast-paced turbulent world.

Ecological breakdown, the trajectory of technological innovation, along with an uncertain and divided political outlook, means that societal influence will play a key role for our current and emerging generations. This rapid change also presents a huge opportunity, as we become more technologically enabled than ever before. AI also presents us with our best chance of avoiding existential threats and it's the current and emerging generations who will possess the knowledge and skills to achieve this.

Governance will play a key role. If we can wisely govern the adoption and use of our increasing AI capability, then we will possess the ability to change the course of our future and the world. Good and thoughtful governance can also help significantly address mis and disinformation, as well as protect users of the Internet from harmful, damaging and explicit content that only serves to sabotage mental well-being and stability. If through the appropriate governance we can address these issues, it will go a long way to slow and de-escalate our increasing polarisation, which is currently dividing society and crippling us through inaction. Better governance can also help breach the echo chambers of conspiracy theories, which will go some way to rebuilding trust and restoring our relationships with truth, information, tolerance and institution.

Current and emerging generations will, without question, face a turbulent economic and financial outlook. With education, housing and our basic cost of living rising to unaffordable levels for many people, we must find solutions to help support younger people to flourish and thrive, whilst also understanding that these are issues that every previous generation has faced to a greater or lesser degree.

Finally, as a society we must understand that in the history of evolution, never has anything which has come before been an adaptation of what followed. Evolution only works through adaptations of prior organisms, meaning that for our older generations who view their younger counterparts as inadequate or believe that they should be more like their younger selves, it's simply not going to happen. Nor should it. Indeed, we must take our share of shouldering the burden of the next generation's pain and pleasure, because it's us, our genetics, parental influence and the societies we created that has caused this adaptation. However, ultimately it is our responsibility to better understand their world, their future and commit to supporting and enabling them in the best way we can.

No, "they don't make them like they used to", they are made differently, for a different world that we helped create.

Educational Influence – the future, efficacy and effectiveness of education and learning.

Given advances in digital capability, its impact and influence on how modern generations learn, there are now urgent and important questions around the efficacy and effectiveness of our current educational system. Is it moving and progressing at the same rate as societal and generational shift? Is it fit for purpose? Do we need to re-think subject matter and its appropriateness? Is it preparing our children for the world they will inherit?

In January 2020 the World Economic Forum published a report on the future of schooling and education. Entitled *Schools of the Future: Defining New Models of Education for the Fourth Industrial Revolution*[54] the report's main message is that in creating future fit-for-purpose education systems we need to, not simply prepare for and adjust to the societal and environmental changes that appear most likely, but also for the ones we're not expecting. So how should we do this? The report sets out four scenarios for the future of education:

Scenario 1. SCHOOLING EXTENDED – Participation in formal education continues to expand. International collaboration and technological advances support more individualised learning. The main structures and process of traditional schooling remain.

Scenario 2. EDUCATION OUTSOURCED – Traditional schooling systems break down, as society becomes more directly involved in educating its citizens. Learning takes place through more diverse, privatised and flexible arrangements, with digital technology being the key driver.

Scenario 3. SCHOOLS AS LEARNING HUBS – Schools remain, but diversity and experimentation have become the norm. "Opening the school walls" connects schools to their communities, favouring ever-changing forms of learning, civic engagement and social innovation.

Scenario 4. LEARN-AS-YOU-GO – Education takes place everywhere, anytime. Distinctions between formal and informal learning are no longer valid as society relies entirely on the power of information technology.

It will be fascinating to watch how education evolves to keep pace with the change we are experiencing generationally and technologically. I feel, certainly in the UK, we'll see a Schooling Extended approach for at least the next 15 to 20 years, with continuous innovations being applied within that formal system. However, with so many young people already struggling within this system, educational institutions will have a challenging time making the adjustments required to support students with their physical and mental health. That said, we still have one of the most advanced, robust and successful educational systems in the world.

Pain and Pleasure — the everlasting, inevitable and unquestionable aspect of being human…

My aim in writing this book was to set out and deliver over 20 years of my learning, experience and findings around human behaviour and the psychology behind how we think, feel, act and behave, validating these findings with the most up-to-date research in neuroscience, psychology and biology. However, over and above this I wanted to write a highly relatable and readable book that not only draws attention to the balancing act we humans need to address, but also delivers personal insight, tools and techniques to help make life more productive and content.

So, to conclude, let's replay the main points one last time. Take some time to reflect on them in combination with your earlier testing results from Chapters 3, 4 and 5. If you haven't taken up the opportunity to take the tests, please do, it will enhance your self-knowledge and support all the techniques we've been exploring.

As you reflect, look for the opportunities to help balance your pain and pleasure scales: this balance is without doubt the key to enjoying a more fulfilled and happy life.

Key points revisited....

The Three Core Functions of Existence
We humans have evolved over millions of years based on the three core functions that we all share as a species.

- **Survival** – I must stay alive and self-preserve at all costs.

- **Reproduction** – I must find a mate and reproduce in order to continue the species.

- **Purpose** – I must have a role or purpose.

Our neurological system is based on pain and pleasure to motivate us away from pain, discomfort and danger, or towards pleasure, reward and fulfilment.

The Three Psychological States
Given that we have three core functions of existence governed by our pain and pleasure system, we can be in one of three psychological states at any one time:

- **Neutral State** – avoid pain, seek comfort.
- **Challenge State** – seek pleasure, endure pain.
- **Threat State** – avoid immediate danger or threat.

Developing the ability to recognise when we are in each of our states, and what it looks and feels like, and then develop the ability to operate within each of them effectively and switch accordingly, will allow us to better balance our pain and pleasure scales.

High vs Low Road Dilemma
In order to balance our states accordingly we need to get better at choosing High Road and Low Road situations and resist the temptation of taking continuous Low Road options.

- Low Road motivation – short-term immediate relief, results, gains or gratification.

- High Road motivation – long-term delayed relief, results, gains or gratification.

In a world full of Low Road motivation options, we must recognise when we are in a perpetual cycle of comfort and ease. Pushing into High Road motivation situations is critical for building competence, confidence and resilience. It's essential for entering the Challenge State mindset, which in turn raises our overall resilience threshold, better equipping us for dealing with the Threat State when it arrives.

Nature and Nurture

Although, as a species we all share the three core functions of human existence, we are all weirdly unique and wonderful when it comes to our personality types, characteristics and traits. This is because of the complex combination between our nature and nurture.

- Our nature is governed by the biochemistry we have inherited: the mix of genes from our mothers and fathers.

- Our nurture is developed by cognitive programming through exposure to our environment: our external experiences and influences mainly, parental, social and educational.

So, by being able to identify what our natural traits, attributes and characteristics are, it means we can be far more self-aware and better understand our strengths, whilst identifying areas we can build on. There are plenty of psychometric tests available to help us do this. Here at T2 we recommend a range of tests, including OCEAN, PRINT® profiling and The Attributes Assessment™ tool.

Your World View

A World View has two distinct parts: the first is our current mental model of how the world is organised, structured and works. It's our unique perceived framework for how the world operates. The second is how much, or how little, we buy into or agree with that framework.

I have given you some of the individual elements that make up a world view in Chapter 4. Other elements are widely debated in the psychology community, but understanding what your views are on the big five questions listed in this book will give you an indication of the way you are likely to see the world, and to what degree you believe it is aligned with reality. Your world view is incredibly important to reflect upon, as in my experience, quite often a world view can be the root cause behind your worries, anxieties and frustrations. Ask yourself the question: Is your world view serving you well and how many of its elements constitute an internal versus external locus of control? Remember, the key lies within the balance.

Enduring Pain and Seeking Pleasure

We explored the key attributes and characteristics for enduring pain and discomfort whilst seeking pleasure and reward. Think about the Attributes™ testing in Chapter 5, those you scored highly on and those that were moderate or low scores. There is no good or bad, right or wrong attribute, it's about bringing in more awareness to them and working on the lower scoring attributes to support yourself in situations where you need them most.

Balancing the Scales

Finally, we turned the spotlight on the fact that we, as a species, have tipped the pain-pleasure scales out of balance. Many of us are living in a "comfort crisis", fuelled by an unending cycle of Low Road motivation and far too much time spent in our Neutral State, ill equipping us to push into Challenge or Threat State effectively and productively. This repeating pattern is altering the way our dopamine system operates, leading to an inability to experience pleasure in the way it was evolutionarily programmed to operate, whilst also sabotaging our ability to endure pain and discomfort when faced with the hardships of life.

If our species is going to successfully dominate and evolve for another 100,000 years on Earth, then I believe we must balance our pain-pleasure scales accordingly.

We must rediscover and develop our ability to endure pain and discomfort, whilst possessing the ability to seek out and experience pleasure and reward.

Simply put,

we must get back to being human.

Acknowledgements

Firstly, I would like to thank Jacky Fitt and Ned Hoste of Big Ideas Library for supporting me with the writing and design of this book. You are both amazing to work with.

To Lucy, my wife, thank you for your ongoing and unwavering support of everything I do. I love you very much.

Thanks must also go to Rich Diviney for agreeing to write the foreword to this book and for his input and encouragement throughout. Rich, your council and mentorship is greatly appreciated.

Finally, to the many people I meet and support through my work – we're all on a journey together and we'll get there! Most of all, I want to thank my team here at T2. Your hard work and commitment keep me balanced. I could not do this work on my own. It takes a team to make a difference and we have the best team I could wish for.

Martin

About the Author

Following five years' military service, Martin has carried out senior sales and leadership roles in both small dynamic and large global organisations, including seven years with global consulting giant, Gartner. He is now the Founder and CEO of Trans2 Performance and is highly regarded for his expertise in Organisational Culture, Organisational Design, Leadership and Human Performance. Over the past few years, Martin has become a strategic advisor and a leading performance coach, who has worked with large corporations within both the private and public sectors, the military and in the world of professional sport. Martin has worked with the likes of Sir Dave Brailsford, former Navy SEAL Commander Rich Diviney and organisations including; Amazon Prime, Specsavers and HSBC.

If you have enjoyed this book

I Am Human 30 Mistakes to Success lifts the lid on 30 of the most common subconscious mistakes and missed opportunities that we humans fail to correct or take advantage of.

"Martin's knowledge and insight have helped us create our organisational culture."
Carolyn Woolway,
Siemens Gamesa

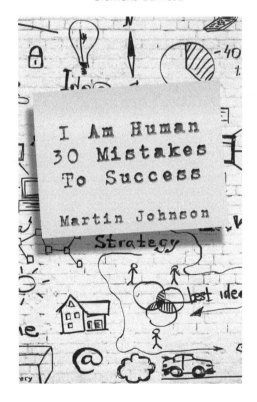

AVAILABLE TO ORDER ON AMAZON TODAY

Endnotes

[1] There is research around a third 'freeze' response to accompany 'fight or flight'. Some believe this to be a more consciously driven response, for my purposes I am simplifying it to 'fight or flight'.

[2] *Ancient genomes show social and reproductive behaviour of early Upper Palaeolithic foragers.* Science (5th October 2017) Vol 358, Issue 6363 pp. 659-662
https://www.science.org/doi/10.1126/science.aao1807

[3] Charles Darwin, author of *On the Origin of Species* (1859)

[4] *Dopamine Nation: Find Balance in the Age of Indulgence* by Dr Anna Lembke, Headline Publishing Group (2021) ISBN: 9781472294159

[5] *The Comfort Crisis: Embrace Discomfort To Reclaim Your Wild, Happy, Healthy Self* by Michael Easter, Rodale Books (2021) ISBN-10: 0593138767

[6] Andrew Huberman is an American podcaster and neuroscientist, an associate professor of neurobiology and ophthalmology at Stanford University School of Medicine. Host of the Huberman Lab podcast.

[7] *Early Experiences Can Alter Gene Expression and Affect Long-Term Development:* Working Paper No. 10. National Scientific Council on the Developing Child (2010).
www.developingchild.harvard.edu.

[8] *Researchers discover group of genes that influence pain and brain communication can also influence alcohol use disorder risk* Indiana School of Medicine (July 2023)
https://medicine.iu.edu/news/2023/07/aud-gene-group-discovery

9   Stephen Hawking was an English theoretical physicist, cosmologist and author, and Lucasian Professor of Mathematics at Cambridge, one of the most prestigious academic posts in the world.
https://en.wikipedia.org/wiki/Stephen_Hawking

10   Lucius Annaeus Seneca was a leading intellectual figure in Rome in the mid-1st century CE. Seneca was a philosopher, statesman, orator and tragedian.

11   Hermann Karl Hesse was a German-Swiss poet, novelist, and painter. His best-known works all explore an individual's search for authenticity, self-knowledge, and spirituality.

12   *My Stroke of Insight: A Brain Scientist's Personal Journey* by Dr Jill Bolte Taylor, a Harvard-trained neuroanatomist. The book charts Bolte Taylor's experience of recovery from a stroke. She shares insights on brain function, mindfulness and the power of the human spirit. Hodder & Stoughton (2009) ISBN: 9780340980507

13   Nelson Mandela was a South African anti-apartheid activist and politician who served as the first president of South Africa from 1994 to 1999. He was the country's first black head of state and the first elected in a fully representative democratic election.

14   Woody Hayes was an influential and highly successful American football player and coach and one of the first major college head coaches to recruit African American players.

15   *I Am Human: 30 Mistakes to Success* by Martin Johnson, Big Ideas Library (2017) ISBN: 9780992985981

16   Billy Jean King is a former no. 1 world tennis player and champion for social justice and gender equality.

17   *Mental Representation and Mental Practice: Experimental Investigation on the Functional Links between Motor Memory and Motor Imagery* by Cornelia Frank, William M. Land, Carmen Popp, Thomas Schack (April 17th 2014)
https://doi.org/10.1371/journal.pone.0095175

[18] *Mental Practice Combined With Physical Practice for Upper-Limb Motor Deficit in Subacute Stroke* by Stephen J Page, Peter Levine, Sue Ann Sisto, Mark V. Johnston
Physical Therapy, Volume 81, Issue 8, (1 August 2001) Pages 1455-1462
https://doi.org/10.1093/ptj/81.8.1455

[19] Nelson Mandela was a South African anti-apartheid activist and politician who served as the first president of South Africa from 1994 to 1999. He was the country's first black head of state and the first elected in a fully representative democratic election.

[20] International Civil Aviation Organization (ICAO) Safety Report 2022
https://www.icao.int/safety/Documents/ICAO_SR_2022.pdf

[21] International Air Transport Association (IATA) 2022 Airline Safety Performance Report
https://www.iata.org/en/pressroom/2023-releases/2023-03-07-01/

[22] "The Problem of Generations" Karl Mannheim
https://en.wikipedia.org/wiki/Theory_of_generations

[23] Alexis Abramson PhD, gained her Doctorate in Gerontology from University of Southern California and has dedicated over 25 years to multi-generational studies and the science of aging.
https://alexisabramson.com

[24] UK office of national statistics (ONS) the UK's largest independent producer of official statistics and its recognised national statistical institute, responsible for collecting and publishing statistics related to the economy, population and society at national, regional and local levels.
https://www.ons.gov.uk

[25] UK office of national statistics (ONS) the UK's largest independent producer of official statistics and its recognised national statistical institute, responsible for collecting and publishing statistics related to the economy, population and society at national, regional and local levels.
https://www.ons.gov.uk

[26] Summer of Love: a social phenomenon of 1967 in the US when around 100,000 people converged in Haight-Ashbury, San Francisco. The lure of experimenting with sexual freedom and drugs and renouncing more conservative social values stemming from an alternative youth culture that had been emerging throughout Europe and America for some years.

[27] ResearchGate connects the world of science and make research open to all. The 20 million researchers in the online community come from diverse sectors in over 190 countries, and use ResearchGate to connect, collaborate, and share their work.
https://www.researchgate.net

[28] Pew Research Centre: a nonpartisan fact tank that informs the public about the issues, attitudes and trends shaping the world, conducting public opinion polling, demographic research, content analysis and other data-driven social science research.
https://www.pewresearch.org

[29] The Council on Foreign Relations (CFR), a US independent, nonpartisan membership organisation, think tank, and publisher, founded in 1921. *Major Epidemics of the Modern Era*:
https://www.cfr.org/timeline/major-epidemics-modern-era

[30] Pew Research Centre: a nonpartisan fact tank that informs the public about the issues, attitudes and trends shaping the world, conducting public opinion polling, demographic research, content analysis and other data-driven social science research.
https://www.pewresearch.org

[31] American Psychological Association (APA) (2018) survey: *Stress in America™: Generation Z*
https://www.apa.org/news/press/releases/stress/2018/stress-gen-z.pdf

[32] *Two million commercially insured Americans diagnosed with major depression are not seeking any treatment* by Blue Cross, Blue Shield, data-driven insight: March 2019
https://www.bcbs.com/the-health-of-america/articles/two-million-commercially-insured-americans-diagnosed-major-depression-not-seeking-treatment

[33] *A Tsunami of Learners Called Generation Z* by Darla Rothman PhD (2016)
https://ce.wvu.edu/media/15624/needs-different_learning_styles.pdf

[34] *5 Reasons Generation Z will be 'Generation Smart' about College* by Andrew Josuweit, Forbes Magazine 2018
https://www.forbes.com/sites/andrewjosuweit/2018/03/21/5-reasons-generation-z-will-be-generation-smart-about-college/

[35] *Generation Z is missing out on the benefits of sex* byJustin J Lehmiller PhD Psychology Today 2022
https://www.psychologytoday.com/gb/blog/the-myths-sex/202209/generation-z-is-missing-out-the-benefits-sex

[36] Margaret Mead was a US-born influential cultural anthropologist, author and speaker.

[37] *Do Mobile Phones Cause Cancer?* Cancer Research UK (2024) https://www.cancerresearchuk.org/about-cancer/causes-of-cancer/cancer-myths/do-mobile-phones-cause-cancer

[38] *Wakefield's article linking MMR vaccine and autism was fraudulent* British Medical Journal (2011)
https://doi.org/10.1136/bmj.c7452

[39] Winston Churchill was Prime Minister of the United Kingdom from 1940 to 1945 during World War II and again from 1951 to 1955.

[40] *Look Again: The Power of Noticing What was Already There* by Tali Sharot and Cass R. Sunstein Bridge Street Press (2024) ISBN: 9780349128764

[41] *What is an intermittent fasting diet?* By Sarah Lienard BBC Good Food Guide (2023)
https://www.bbcgoodfood.com/howto/guide/what-intermittent-fasting-diet

[42] *How Emotions Are Made: The Secret Life of the Brain* by Lisa Feldman Barratt Pan, (2018) ISBN: 9781509837526

[43] *Brief Intense Stair Climbing Improves Cardiorespiratory Fitness* by Mary K. Allison, Jessica H. Baglole, Brian J. Martin, Martin J. Macinnis, Brendon J. Gurd, Martin J. Gibala Medicine & Science in Sports & Exercise p 298-307, (February 2017). I DOI: 10.1249/ MSS.0000000000001188

https://journals.lww.com/acsm-msse/Fulltext/2017/02000/Brief_ Intense_Stair_Climbing_Improves.10.aspx

[44] Industrialist Elisha Otis installed the first passenger elevator in New York and held a public demonstration at the 1854 world's fair in New York

https://edition.cnn.com/style/article/short-history-of-the-elevator/ index.html

[45] Research commissioned by OnePoll on behalf of Ninja Kitchen, (May 2022), representative 2,000 UK respondents
https://ninjakitchen.co.uk/fast-food-cms-page.takeaway

[46] *Money Waste UK* by Raisin (2023) www.raisin.co.uk
https://www.raisin.co.uk/newsroom/raisin-research/money-waste-uk/#:~:text=Unused%20gym%20memberships,200%20for%20 the%20average%20household

[47] *The Health Benefits of Socialising* by Angela K. Troyer Ph.D., C.Psych. Psychology Today June (2016)
https://www.psychologytoday.com/gb/blog/living-mild-cognitive-impairment/201606/the-health-benefits-socializing#:~:text=Research%20has%20shown%20that%20 one,good%20for%20your%20brain%20health.

[48] Indeed UK Workplace Happiness Survey 2022
https://uk.indeed.com/career-advice/career-development/work-happiness-survey

[49] Susan Jeffers, author of the best-selling book *Feel the Fear and Do It Anyway* is an American psychologist.
https://susanjeffers.com

50 Lewis Pugh is a British born endurance swimmer, a UN Patron of the Oceans and maritime lawyer. The first person to undertake a long-distance swim in every ocean of the world.
www.lewispugh.com

51 The Health Foundation is an independent UK grant-making charity seeking to bring about better health and healthcare in the UK.
https://www.health.org.uk/

52 The Resolution Foundation is a UK independent think-tank working across a wide range of economic and social policy with a commitment to analytical rigour.
https://www.resolutionfoundation.org/

53 *We've Only Just Begun: Action to improve young people's mental health, education and employment* by Charlie McCurdy & Louise Murphy Resolution Foundation (2024)
https://www.resolutionfoundation.org/publications/weve-only-just-begun/

54 *Schools of The Future: Defining New Models of Education for the Fourth Industrial Revolution* World Economic Forum (January 2020)
https://www.weforum.org/publications/schools-of-the-future-defining-new-models-of-education-for-the-fourth-industrial-revolution/

Further Reading

Sapiens: A Brief History of Humankind by Yuval Noah Harari
Vintage Publishing (2015) ISBN: 9780099590088

On the Origin of Species by Charles Darwin with introduction by Peter Garrett
Flame Tree Publishing (2019) ISBN: 9781787556805

The Chimp Paradox: The Acclaimed Mind Management Programme to Help You Achieve Success, Confidence and Happiness by Professor Steve Peters
Ebury Publishing (2012) ISBN: 9780091935580

The Comfort Crisis: Embrace Discomfort To Reclaim Your Wild, Happy, Healthy Self by Michael Easter Potter/Ten Speed/Harmony/Rodale (2021) ISBN: 9780593138762

Dopamine Nation: Find Balance in the Age of Indulgence by Dr Anna Lembke Headline Publishing Group (2023) ISBN: 9781472294159

My Stroke of Insight: A Brain Scientist's Personal Journey by Dr Jill Bolte Taylor Hodder & Stoughton (2009) ISBN: 9780340980507

I Am Human 30: Mistakes to Success by Martin Johnson, Big Ideas Library (2017) ISBN: 9780992985981

The Attributes: 25 Hidden Drivers of Optimal Performance by Rich Diviney Random House (2021) ISBN: 9780593133941

Look Again: the Power of Noticing What was Already There by Tali Sharot and Cass R. Sunstein, Bridge Street Press, (2024) ISBN: 9780349128764

How Emotions Are Made: The Secret Life of the Brain by Lisa Feldman Barratt, Pan (2018) ISBN: 9781509837526